THE TALE OF
Mrs WILLIAM HEELIS
BEATRIX POTTER

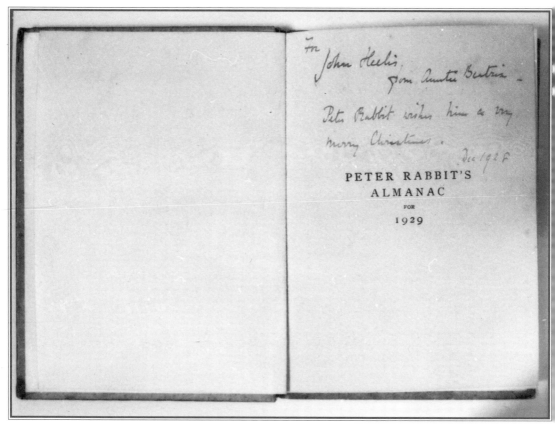

Peter Rabbit's Almanac dedicated by Beatrix to the author.

THE TALE OF Mrs WILLIAM HEELIS BEATRIX POTTER

JOHN HEELIS

SUTTON PUBLISHING

First published by Leading Edge Press & Publishing Ltd
This new revised and reillustrated edition first published in the United
Kingdom in 1999 by
Sutton Publishing Limited · Phoenix Mill
Thrupp · Stroud · Gloucestershire · GL5 2BU

British Library Cataloguing in Publication Data
A catalogue record for this book is available from the British Library.

ISBN 0-7509-2125-0

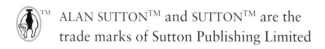 ALAN SUTTON™ and SUTTON™ are the
trade marks of Sutton Publishing Limited

Typeset in 11/15 pt Sabon.
Typesetting and origination by
Sutton Publishing Limited.
Printed in Great Britain by
Redwood Books, Trowbridge, Wiltshire.

CONTENTS

LIST OF ILLUSTRATIONS

FOREWORD

Michael Hemming, *Chairman of the Beatrix Potter Society*

Beatrix Potter is Mrs William Heelis. She lives in the north of England, her home is among the mountains and lakes that she has drawn in her picture books. Her husband is a lawyer.

These words, written by Beatrix Potter in 1925 in response to a request from America for biographical details, illustrate how firmly the author of the 'Peter Rabbit' tales had come to identify herself with the man she married in 1913 at the age of forty-seven and with whom she was to spend the happiest and most fulfilled years of her life.

Through Beatrix Potter's letters we can sense her husband to be a devoted and steadfast companion, steeped in his forebears' way of life and dedicated both to his legal practice and to his sporting interests; always ready to support his wife's endeavours and to offer her the benefit of his advice. Photographs of William Heelis show a kindly, serious and thoughtful man, with just a twinkle in the corner of his eye revealing a sense of humour hidden not far below the surface – the epitome of the conscientious north-country professional gentleman serving the community in which he lived and worked.

The Heelises were an extensive family and well known throughout the old counties of Westmorland and Cumberland. They were respectable and hard-working, most of their male members being land agents, lawyers or clergymen. Traces of their presence remain to this day – in the belltower of Hawkshead Church, for example, there is a plaque bearing the name of W.D. Heelis, William's cousin and partner in their law firm, who was churchwarden in 1911.

However, it was not until John Heelis, William's great-nephew, embarked on a long and painstaking programme of research into his ancestors that we were able to gain detailed first-hand knowledge of the Heelis family and its roots. He has traced his direct family line as far back as the early 1600s and indirectly back to 1560. His efforts have uncovered a wealth of fascinating material and his recollections and those of his relations throw fresh and intriguing light on to the close and affectionate partnership between Beatrix Potter and her husband.

Judy Taylor, my predecessor as Chairman of the Beatrix Potter Society, provided the foreword to the first edition of this book, and I consider it a great pleasure and a privilege to have been asked to follow in her footsteps. As Judy remarked in the first edition, 'the story of Beatrix Potter has been well studied and widely disseminated. Now we can add to the story of Mrs Beatrix Heelis and, most importantly, that of her husband, Willie.'

THE HEELIS FAMILY TREE

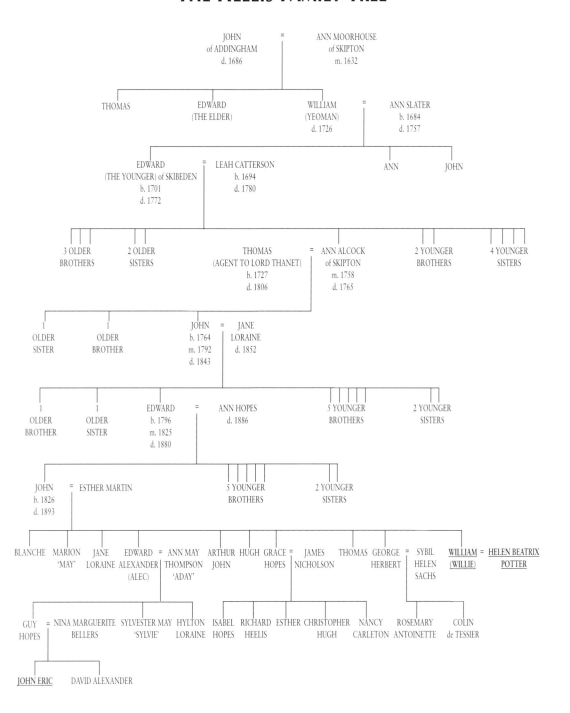

JOHN
of ADDINGHAM
d. 1686
=
ANN MOORHOUSE
of SKIPTON
m. 1632

THOMAS

EDWARD
(THE ELDER)

WILLIAM
(YEOMAN)
d. 1726
=
ANN SLATER
b. 1684
d. 1757

EDWARD
(THE YOUNGER) of SKIBEDEN
b. 1701
d. 1772
=
LEAH CATTERSON
b. 1694
d. 1780

ANN

JOHN

3 OLDER
BROTHERS

2 OLDER
SISTERS

THOMAS
(AGENT TO LORD THANET)
b. 1727
d. 1806
=
ANN ALCOCK
of SKIPTON
m. 1758
d. 1765

2 YOUNGER
BROTHERS

4 YOUNGER
SISTERS

1
OLDER
SISTER

1
OLDER
BROTHER

JOHN
b. 1764
m. 1792
d. 1843
=
JANE
LORAINE
d. 1852

1
OLDER
BROTHER

1
OLDER
SISTER

EDWARD
b. 1796
m. 1825
d. 1880
=
ANN HOPES
d. 1886

5 YOUNGER
BROTHERS

2 YOUNGER
SISTERS

JOHN
b. 1826
d. 1893
=
ESTHER MARTIN

5 YOUNGER
BROTHERS

2 YOUNGER
SISTERS

BLANCHE MARION
'MAY'

JANE
LORAINE

EDWARD
ALEXANDER
(ALEC)
=
ANN MAY
THOMPSON
'ADAY'

ARTHUR HUGH
JOHN

GRACE
HOPES
=
JAMES
NICHOLSON

THOMAS GEORGE
HERBERT
=
SYBIL
HELEN
SACHS

WILLIAM
(WILLIE)
=
HELEN BEATRIX
POTTER

GUY
HOPES
=
NINA MARGUERITE
BELLERS

SYLVESTER MAY
'SYLVIE'

HYLTON
LORAINE

ISABEL
HOPES

RICHARD
HEELIS

ESTHER CHRISTOPHER
HUGH

NANCY
CARLETON

ROSEMARY
ANTOINETTE

COLIN
de TESSIER

JOHN ERIC

DAVID ALEXANDER

INTRODUCTION AND ACKNOWLEDGEMENTS

Like so many boys of my generation and, I am glad to say, of succeeding generations too, my earliest memories of the books read to me, and which I later read to myself, were the 'little books' of Beatrix Potter.

For many years I worked on a short history of the Heelis family, involving a lot of research and correspondence with my relations while their memory still served. It was never intended for publication, just as a labour of love as head of the family for their interest only. I recently completed a final edition and sent out copies to all the family who were interested. I included two chapters on the two best-known people who were connected with the Heelis family – G.L. Stampa and Beatrix Potter. Cousin Georgie drew cockney urchins and many other drawings for *Punch* for over fifty years. A biography by his granddaughter, Flavia Stampa-Gruss, entitled *The Last of the Bohemians*, was published by Bellew of London in 1991. I received great help for my chapter on Great Aunt Beatrix from Margaret Lane's books and the correspondence between her and Great Uncle Willie's trustees after his death. (I shall refer to William Heelis as 'Willie' throughout as that is how he was always known to us.) Further information became available to me with the publication of Leslie Linder's excellent books *The Art of Beatrix Potter* (Warne, 1955), and *A History of the Writings of Beatrix Potter* (Warne, 1971).

Then one happy day in the 1980s my late wife and I received a visit from Judy Taylor and her husband. Judy, at that time Chairman of the Beatrix Potter Society, was busy researching for her book *Beatrix Potter: Artist, Storyteller and Countrywoman* and for the 'Letters' book that was to follow. Thus began a sincere friendship and a steady flow of correspondence between us. Shortly afterwards I joined the Beatrix Potter Society and found myself delving even deeper into the family records, and talking to people still around who had known Mr and Mrs Willie Heelis. I also paid several visits to the Hawkshead area to track down the various houses in which members of the Heelis family had lived. In 1990 I found myself giving a talk on Beatrix Potter – Mrs Heelis – at the fourth biennial Beatrix Potter Society study conference at Brockhole beside Lake Windermere. The interest this created encouraged me in this attempt to put on record some of what I had found out about the Heelis family into which Beatrix Potter had married, most of which had been undocumented up to now.

In this new edition I have included some of the additional information that has come to light since the book's first publication in 1993. I am most grateful to the many people who have written to me.

I have also included a few extracts from letters recently given to the Victoria and Albert Museum by my cousin, Nancy Hudson, which were written by Beatrix to Nancy and her mother. I hereby acknowledge with gratitude the granting of permission by the Trustees to use this material, which has not previously been published. The letters are recorded as NN 10 and 11 in the Beatrix Potter collection at the National Art Library.

I am indebted to Michael Hemming for his generous foreword to this edition. He is well qualified to write it both as the dedicated National Trust Curator of Hill Top for many years and as Chairman of the Beatrix Potter Society.

I also acknowledge with gratitude the help I have received in the continuity of my story from the books of Margaret Lane, Leslie Linder, Judy Taylor and W.R. Mitchell, the kindness and encouragement given by fellow members of the Beatrix Potter Society on both sides of the Atlantic, and from Anne Hobbs, Nancy Hudson, Sylvia Usher, Ann Fearnhill, Joan Meschede, Anne Lysaght, George Forrester, Josephine Banner, Joe Hodgson, Amanda Thistlethwaite, Molly Green, Willow Taylor, Mrs Macon, Nigel Jee (for the Louie Choyce letters), Susan Denyer of the National Trust, Marion Longthorn of Skipton, the *Westmorland Gazette*, the Trustees of the Victoria and Albert Museum, the staff of Frederick Warne & Co. and The Dalesman Publishing Company.

CHAPTER ONE

BEATRIX MARRIES WILLIE HEELIS

Beatrix Potter married Willie Heelis at St Mary Abbot's Church, Kensington, on 15 October 1913. In spite of the fact that her parents had previously disapproved of the marriage, Rupert and Helen Potter attended the ceremony and signed the register. The other witnesses were Gertrude M. Woodward, an old friend of Beatrix's and the daughter of Dr Henry Woodward, keeper of Geology at the British Museum, and Willie's cousin, Lelio Stampa, an Oxford don, whose mother had been a Heelis. Lelio Stampa and his brother George Loraine Stampa were educated at Appleby Grammar School, which many of Willie's other Heelis relatives also attended. Cousin Georgie was a *Punch* artist, working for that journal for over fifty years.

Much has been written about Beatrix's early life in London, her visits to Scotland, the Lakes and sometimes the seaside with her parents and brother Bertram; also about her writings and her artistic ability, but very little about the Heelis family of which she had now become a member. For a long time Beatrix had despaired of ever obtaining permission from her parents to marry Willie, as they considered a country solicitor beneath Rupert Potter's status of barrister. Just a month before the wedding however Beatrix wrote to a friend: 'William has actually been invited up for a weekend soon – they never say much, but they cannot dislike him.'

It is not so generally known that Willie's sisters at Appleby also disapproved of his choice of Beatrix. While acknowledging that her father was a barrister, they felt that the Potter family background was trade and dissenter while the Heelis family were yeomen, Church of England and the professions. Perhaps they did not voice their disapproval as vehemently as the Potters, but there were undoubtedly whisperings behind closed doors.

The *Westmorland Gazette* of 17 October 1913, records the event as follows:

In the quietest of quiet manners two very well-known local inhabitants were married in London on Wednesday. The two parties to this most interesting wedding were Mr W. Heelis of Hawkshead Hall and Miss Helen Beatrix Potter of Hill Top, Sawrey. None of their friends knew of the wedding, which was solemnized in the simplest form, characteristic of such modest though accomplished bridegroom and bride.

Mr Heelis is the son of the late Rev John Heelis. He comes of one of the most athletic and sporting County families. He himself is one of the best all-round sportsmen in the Lake District. There is hardly a finer shot in the countryside. He is a keen angler. The bride is a successful exhibitor at local agricultural shows of shorthorn cattle and her name is known now all over the country for those charming books for children which have become so deservedly popular.

Quite soon of course, Beatrix came to be accepted and admired by the Heelis family, though she generally got on better with the men than with their wives. She was particularly good with the children, and generous with financial help when it was needed. She helped to pay for the education of several of them and took great interest in their progress.

The oft-told story of Beatrix dressed in her usual working clothes meeting a tramp on the road, who greeted her with the words, 'Sad weather for the likes of thee and me,' is matched by a comment from the wife of Willie's partner, William Dickenson Heelis, who went to visit some friends in Sawrey before Willie and Beatrix were engaged. She met a woman in the drive with pattens on her feet and a shawl over her head, carrying a butter basket with flowers in it. She assumed her to be a woman from the village. She was astonished when friends asked her if she had met Miss Potter on the way to them. 'No,' said Mrs W.D. 'Well, she's just been here with a bunch of flowers,' the friends replied. The Hawkshead cousins described her as usually wearing an old black hat, a thick tweed coat and skirt and black woollen stockings with clogs or black laced boots. If there was an agricultural show you would be sure to find her hanging over a sheep pen.

It was considered a bit of a joke among the Hawkshead Heelises that when Willie and Beatrix came back from their marriage there was a white bull calf in the back of the car. Beatrix Moore, the daughter of her old governess, remembered being highly amused when Willie and Beatrix visited her while still on their honeymoon in London and told her that their first priority on returning home would be to meet a new bull at the railway

Beatrix Potter and Willie Heelis, an engagement photograph.

Beatrix and Willie on their wedding day.

station. It is also said that Willie and his new bride nearly set off on the wrong train from London after their honeymoon, having, as they thought, got on the Penrith train, only to discover just in time that they were about to set off to Penarth in Wales. Comments in Sawrey village at the time included, 'I'd never thought we'd get Miss Potter off our hands,' and, 'I wonder if he'll give up the office now. Happen he'll be glad to have an office to go to.'

W.D. Heelis's daughter, Sylvia, recalls that her father, although Willie's partner, never visited Willie and Beatrix at Castle Cottage. Sylvia's mother only actually met Beatrix once when she called to ask what she would like for a wedding present. Whatever she suggested did not seem to suit, so finally in desperation she suggested a silver cream jug. 'If you give me a silver cream jug I'll throw it out of the window, I can't abide them,' was

Lelio Stampa, one of the witnesses at Beatrix's wedding.

Beatrix's reply. Sylvia also remembers an incident before she married her husband, George Usher. A relation was ill and needed a wheelchair. Beatrix said she had one and Sylvia was sent to fetch it. It was at least a 2-mile journey and it was an old-fashioned cumbersome affair, not easy to wheel on one's own. However, Sylvia struggled off with it and was pushing it up a hill not far from her destination when a friend drew up in his car and offered to help. Beatrix arrived on the scene at that moment and told Sylvia's friend to 'let her be'.

She was tough and forbidding when she thought it necessary, and often seemed lost in her own thoughts, passing people by, head down, without a word. On the other hand I have heard from so many sources of her kindness and generosity, invariably linked with the strict instructions that nothing was to be said about it. It is generally known that she was instrumental in getting the district nurse into the area. It is perhaps not so well known that she provided the first nurse's house and bought her a car. Nurse Edwards came every day to Beatrix for instructions and information

Willie playing bowls.

as to who was ill and needed visiting. Only later was Beatrix persuaded to get together a League of Friends to keep the service going. I have a letter in which she says that she often wished that she had kept the whole District Nursing Association in her own hands as she found it much easier to manage that way.

While most of Willie's brothers and cousins were educated at Appleby Grammar School, he himself went to Sedbergh, as did William Dickenson Heelis. In one of her letters to Willie's niece, Esther Nicholson, Beatrix tells her that Willie kept a ferret in his desk at school. He was brought up a countryman and remained keen on country pursuits all his life. This was of course one of the things about him that appealed to Beatrix. David Beckett, son of Beatrix's mother's coachman, remembers Willie as being a 'fairly tall, rather slim and a perfect gentleman – a country gentleman and a charming man'. Josephine Banner, the wife of Delmar Banner who painted the portrait of Beatrix which hangs in the National Portrait Gallery, described Willie as 'a rather sweet old-fashioned English gentleman, of the kind that one reads about in Dickens and so on. He was very tall and good-looking.'

Early on in their married life Willie and Beatrix went over to Crosthwaite to spend a night with Willie's brother Tom, the vicar there, and his wife, Ada Isabella. Beatrix complained when they were given two single beds saying that she thought a married couple ought to have a double bed. They had to make do with sharing one of the singles. Another bedroom story told in the family is that Beatrix once took a sick piglet into the conjugal bed at Castle Cottage for the night. It is believed to have made a good recovery.

Mrs Rogerson, the housekeeper at Castle Cottage for over thirty years, recalls a sow called Sally, which became quite affectionate and was often in the dining room with Beatrix – it followed her about like a dog and was very clean.

CHAPTER TWO

THE HEELIS FAMILY OF APPLEBY

So, what of this Heelis family of which Beatrix's parents initially disapproved but later came to accept? They originally came over to Westmorland from the Craven district of Yorkshire, and can be traced directly back to John Heelis, yeoman, of Addingham, who married Ann Moorhouse of Skipton in 1632. He died in 1686 having produced three sons, Thomas, Edward and William. The first two died without issue, but William had a son, Edward of Skibeden, who married Leah, the daughter of Mr Stephen Catterson, an Attorney-at-law and a member of a well-known Skipton family. Edward and Leah's son, Thomas, born in 1727, was Willie Heelis's great-great-grandfather. Leah had two brothers, Francis and Sylvester. The widow of the latter lived to be 101. Leah's great-great-grandfather was Thomas Catterson, 1579–1612, who had land in Skipton from the Earl of Thanet, which is now the Red Lion Inn in the High Street. Leah's maternal grandmother was a Pettit, or Pettyt, another family well documented in the annals of Skipton. Two of her brothers were lawyers at Barnard's Inn in London. One became the chief archivist at the Tower of London, helping to sort out the great medieval treasures stored there. The other continued to practise in London but was a generous benefactor to Skipton, leaving his fine library of books to the town when he died, as well as money for the poor.

Although the Heelises only trace their family tree directly back to the early 1600s, there are a number of entries in the parish registers of Burnsall, Linton-in-Craven and Skipton itself which show members of the family whose relationship cannot exactly be determined, from as far back as at least 1560.

Willie's great-great-grandfather, Thomas, was the agent to the Earl of Thanet at Skipton Castle. His first wife was Ann Alcock of Skipton. He later became the Earl's agent at Appleby Castle in Westmorland, bought property

Thomas Heelis, Willie's great-great-grandfather.

The Revd John Heelis, Willie's great-grandfather.

locally, joined in all local affairs and became the Mayor of Appleby. His second and third wives were Westmorland ladies. When he died Thomas's estate in the Appleby area included land at Crackenthorpe, Bolton and Kirkby Thore, and also at Colby, Hilton and Great Ormside. In Appleby itself he had land at the Brewery and houses adjoining, and in Bongate, Scattergate and Burrells. He also leased some land and had mortgages, securities and livestock.

Thomas's eldest son was the Revd John Heelis, Rector in plurality of Dufton and Brougham in the Eden Valley, at the same time

Jane Heelis (née Loraine), Willie's great-grandmother.

succeeding his father as Lord Thanet's agent. His wife, Jane, from the Loraine family of Northumberland, was a very strong character and many subsequent members of the family have been christened Loraine in her memory. John and Jane lived at Appleby Castle in some style, only turning out when Lord Thanet was in residence. This was not too often as he spent most of his time in London or Hothfield in Kent.

Jane kept detailed inventories of their possessions. In 1841 for example she listed the china belonging to them:

2 soup tureens with deep dishes
1 tureen, 1 dish and 7 dishes besides
9 large china dishes
12 dishes alike
5½ dozen dinner plates
3½ dozen soup plates

In 1848 the 'Plate' was as follows:

2 silver coffee pots
3 tea pots
2 'waters'
1 sugar basin and 3 prs. sugar tongs
1 bread basket
1 ring for the middle of the table
2 prs. candlesticks
18 large forks
18 small forks
18 dessert spoons
30 table spoons
Full set of cut-glass 'castors'
1 cream pitcher
Several prs. candlesticks and snuffers and much else besides.

Jane was thrifty and always adding items to their possessions. Her notebooks record, '1 fish knife got at Leeds. Paid for it for what I made at butter that year', '1 sugar basin made out of coconut, set with silver. Got at the same time and paid for in the same way, with the addition of what I got for a pig' and '1 dry toast rack and a set of spirit castors. Paid for by what I got for pigs'. She also made quilts for their own and the servants' beds: 'several buff-striped made out of J. Heelis's gowns' (for the servants); and '6, all handsewn, striped, blue and white, pink, dark and pattern for the middle' (for her own family). As each of her children went off to other parts of the country she made up linen sheets, bolsters, quilts, feather beds and damask table cloths for them. She was an expert knitter too.

They also ate very well – as the following examples from Jane's account books show:

11th October 1839
100 oysters   2/6d.
3 chickens at 1/- each   3/-
A round beef, 16 lbs. 5½ ozs.   12/-

12th October 1839
A rump of beef, 16 lbs. 5½ ozs.   7/4d.
A leg of veal, 13 lbs, 6½ ozs.   7/-
A goose   4/-

18th October 1839

Fish – 6 haddock	2/3d.
Hindquarters of pork	4/-
Calf feet	6d.

22nd October 1839

Lemons, Mustard	2/8d.
½ stone rice	3/3d.
Flannel waistcoats Wm. Heelis	2/3d.
Cod fish 17 lbs.	2/10d.

2nd November 1839

3 chickens	2/6d.
Leg of Mutton 8½ lbs.	4/-
Muffins	8d.

It was a long way from the coast to Appleby Castle and it seems amazing that they had oysters and seafood regularly, also mussels and cockles frequently. An expensive item was a half chest of tea from London, £12 2s 8d, but a cartload of coal was only 8s 6d.

John often had to buy sheep and cattle at Appleby for Lord Thanet, which were then driven by the drove roads all the way to Kent, invariably arriving safe and well. On 30 May 1808 Lord Thanet wrote to the Revd John Heelis:

Sir, I have ordered some wine to be sent to Appleby by a conveyance. When it arrives I desire you will have it put in the coolest cellar there is in the Castle, and reserve it for my use.

I have heard at this time of the year at Appleby or in the neighbourhood, there are many Scotch wethers four years old to be had. I should be glad if you would get about 150 bought for me. As they would probably be in the wool they might be clipped before they set out on their journey. If you have an opportunity at the same time of getting 40 to 50 Scotch Bullocks they might travel together. Those I had from Roply Hill Fair have turned out uncommonly well.

I am Sir, Your Obedient Servant, Thanet.

Two other letters show that John Heelis's efforts on Lord Thanet's behalf were successful:

24th October 1817 – Hothfield, Kent – The cattle arrived yesterday. Only 4 or 5 appear a little tender in the feet. One of the heifers calved, I understand, early in the journey, but she is come with the others . . . The whole are in very good condition and they appear to me to be as good as any I ever had.

The Revd Edward Heelis, Willie's grandfather.

26th October 1819 – The bullocks arrived here all safe and well . . . Those that had fallen lame on the road got well again in the course of the journey . . .

Willie's grandfather, Edward, the son of the above John and Jane, was the Rector of Long Marton, near Appleby, for forty-two years. It was one of the best livings in the county and he successfully farmed his own glebe. His wife was a Hopes of Stainmore, another name that has recurred as a Christian name in most generations of Heelis since, including William Hopes Heelis of Hawkshead and my father, Guy Hopes Heelis of Appleby.

Long Marton Rectory.

CHAPTER THREE

WILLIE'S GENERATION

Willie's parents were the Revd John Heelis and his wife Esther, a Martin of Patterdale. They had eleven children, Willie being the youngest. The Revd John was first the Rector of Dufton on the East Fellside, and later of Kirkby Thore on the main road between Appleby and Penrith. Willie's eldest sisters, Blanche and May, remained spinsters. The other two both married, Jane to a Dr Jago – they had no children – and Grace to a barrister, James Morton Nicholson, whose daughters often visited Beatrix and Willie, as will be described later. Two brothers, like Willie, were solicitors, and two were parsons. One brother died young, and another farmed in Canada for a time.

The Revd John Heelis used to lay down a pipe of port every year. One year when he was going to bottle it he took all his children down the cellar with him. When their mother came to fetch them, they were all fast asleep – not to say unconscious!

The Revd John Heelis, Willie's father.

They certainly all had to be carried up to bed. The story was put about that they were overcome by the fumes. One wonders whether Willie ever told Beatrix that story about his early life.

They were a close-knit family who went on picnics and fishing parties together and visited each other socially whenever they could. Willie was closest in age to his brother George, who was the junior partner to their eldest brother, Edward Alexander, known as 'Alec' in the Appleby solicitor's office. George and Willie did most things together as young men.

The Heelis family stewardship to the Earls of Thanet continued in the Appleby solicitor's office, and has remained with their successors up to the present day – from its origination with John Heelis of Addingham, who was given a 99-year lease on land at Skibeden in 1652 by Lady Anne Clifford, the illustrious ancestor of the Earls of Thanet and the Tufton family. The lease on this land was twice extended in 1730 and 1760.

Kirkby Thore Rectory.

Willie and his brothers practising golf at Kirkby Thore.

Alec, Arthur John, Willie and George often went shooting together. Some years after marrying Beatrix, Willie's shooting knowledge was used by Beatrix in the unpublished story *Kitty in Boots*. He had to pose for Beatrix to ensure that the gun was held properly. Beatrix also accompanied Willie on fishing expeditions and often used to row the boat when he fished on Moss Eccles Tarn above Sawrey. In a letter to a niece she says: 'Uncle Willie has gone out fishing – or poaching; rather an odd performance occasionally resulting in a 1 lb trout.'

When living at Kirkby Thore, Willie was a member of the village cricket team. He later became a good cricket and tennis player. He and his brothers were early golf players and used to practise in the field behind the

Kirkby Thore cricket team – Willie is fourth from the left, back row.

Rectory at Kirkby Thore. His sister May was one of the earliest members of the Appleby Golf Club and was a good player. Willie continued to be keen on golf after his marriage, becoming a scratch player. In Leslie Linder's account of the writing of *Johnny Town-Mouse* he quotes Mrs Susan Ladbrook as saying that the local doctor, Dr Parsons, was the model for the 'Town-Mouse' and that the 'long bag' he was shown carrying contained golf clubs. She goes on to say: 'When anyone wanted the doctor the villagers would say, "you must find Mr Heelis, they've gone out together with bags of sticks, and where one is you will find the other". Golf was very new then, and few knew anything of the game, but

Willie with his parents, brothers and sisters at Kirkby Thore Rectory. Back row, left to right:
Aday, Thomas, Willie, the Revd John, Blanche, George. Front row: Alec, Esther and Jane.

Dr Parsons and Mr Heelis had a private golf course constructed for their
own use at Sawrey and played together there.'

Willie was also keen on bowling and Beatrix mentioned in one of her
letters discussing the possible construction of a bowling green at Sawrey
with Willie. She wasn't too keen on it, believing that agriculture was more
important. She had also been approached by a Mr Spedding Byers who
wanted to make a green on Heelis land on the southern side of the road
coming over the hill to Sawrey. Beatrix felt it would be an eyesore but
suggested an alternative site on the lower end of the grassy area at Hill Top.
She made it very clear that if she did make a green then it would be for the
use of the public at large and not just for a private bowling association. In
the event it never came to anything. Willie played at Hawkshead and was

Thomas, George and Willie.

later made President of the Hawkshead Bowling Club. He won many cups and medals and was considered a very good player.

Beatrix took a great interest in another of Willie's favourite recreations, folk dancing, a favourite too with his junior partner in the office, Jack Heelis. Willie was also a good swimmer and fond of billiards and indoor games. He was a member of the Volunteers on first arriving in Hawkshead, and later became a Special Constable.

Willie's brother, Thomas, told his sons many years later of what may have been Willie's first swimming lesson. Thomas, a small boy at the time, and some of his older brothers, were setting out for a walk near Appleby with the intention of swimming in the River Eden. They were dismayed when told to take their little brother Willie with them, but there was no getting out of it. When they arrived at their swimming place they thought they had better not leave him on the river bank, so they undressed him and took him in with them. When it came to dressing him again they had some difficulty and although he looked all right on top they found they had some mysterious garment left over. They discussed putting it over the top of everything else, but in the end decided to throw it in the river and hope that it would not be missed among so many clothes.

Willie and Beatrix's cousin Stephanie's husband, Captain Kenneth Duke, had a scheme for trying to net the large number of rabbits that used to come on to the Heelis land – known as The Heights – from a wood belonging to

Alec, his wife Aday and baby son Guy at Kirkby Thore Rectory.

the estate next door. They set the net up near the wood, left it folded while the rabbits passed over it and then slipped the net down to try and catch them running back. The rabbits were too clever for them, and the operation was not very successful.

CHAPTER FOUR

Battlebarrow House, Appleby

M any houses in Appleby and surrounding villages in the Eden Valley belonged at one time or another to members of the Heelis family, but the main one was Battlebarrow House in Appleby itself, converted from an old coaching inn and called The Green. In fact the old bowling green became a croquet lawn, and for many years the ostler's bell still hung above the back door.

It was renamed Battlebarrow House by the Revd Edward Heelis when he and his wife retired from Long Marton, the old house having a new part added at the front. Edward was helped financially in this by the sale of some land for the new Carlisle–Settle railway line which was being built through Appleby at that time. Later Willie's sisters, Blanche and May, lived there, also Jane and Grace before they married. Blanche, May and Grace were very cross when Jane went off to get married as it spoilt their bridge four. Many young Heelises also lodged at Battlebarrow while attending the nearby Grammar School. Uncle Stampa, the father of the *Punch* artist Georgie and of Lelio, the witness at Willie and Beatrix's wedding, lived there after he became a widower.

George Dominic Stampa had married Ann Heelis, Willie's aunt, in 1872. The Stampa family tradition is that the house of Stampa dates back to the time when Pope Leo III confirmed Charlemagne as Emperor. Among the nobles to whom Emperor Charlemagne distributed lands and titles was a Frenchman called Giovanni. He was granted the Castle of Stampa at the foot of Mount Brianza and the Imperial Arms of the Eagle. Uncle Stampa's father had come to England in his youth as a refugee after one of the first risings against the Austrians following the Treaty of Vienna. He himself was born in Constantinople in 1835, and was sent to England to be educated. A pupil of Mr Shepherd at Long Marton Village School, he later qualified as an architect, becoming the official architect to the Sultan of

Ann Stampa, Uncle Stampa, Blanche, George and Willie.

Turkey, and designer of buildings for the Khedive of Egypt. He designed the British Embassy at Therapia, various mosques in and around Constantinople, the Sultan's Palace there, and the Khedive of Egypt's Summer Palace on the Bosporus.

Ann Stampa died in 1915, and George died at Battlebarrow in 1922. He had always looked smart and fashionable. The late Mr Gradwell of Appleby, who used to go to Battlebarrow to cut his hair recalled to me the last time he went there. Uncle Stampa knew he was dying. 'Make a good job of it, Mr Gradwell,' he said, 'I want to look smart in my coffin!'

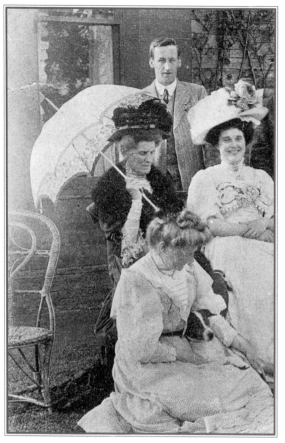

Willie, Ann Stampa, Sybil and May.

Within the memory of some of us still around today, Battlebarrow will always be associated with the truly Dickensian Christmas parties held there every year. Every available Heelis relation traditionally gathered at the house on Christmas Day. Aunt Blanche was very much in charge with the tea urn, assisted by Aunts May, Jane, Grace and Aday (Alec's wife), with the Stampa cousins as house guests. There was a glass screen which Uncle Stampa used to have round him to keep off the draughts, an old horn gramophone, a cabinet full of Indian figures, another of sea shells, and Turkey-red carpets and curtains. The children would be taken through to the breakfast room in the old part of the house through a green baize door, to be told stories and play games with the Stampa cousins.

The Nicholson family, including the five children of Willie's sister, Grace, remembered getting dressed in their best clothes, and their father, James Nicholson, ordering the coachman, Spottiswoode, to yoke up the horse in the old brougham for the journey to Appleby from Kirkby Thore. Off they would trot with the brougham swaying like a ship at sea. On arrival at Battlebarrow the grown-ups were usually just finishing lunch. Coats would be taken upstairs to a bedroom, and then the children led off to the breakfast room. Some games would be organised by cousins Georgie and Lelio Stampa, but most would be in the hands of Aunt May. 'Nuts in May', 'Oranges and Lemons', 'Pounce' or 'Racing Demon' were favourites.

Throughout the afternoon the children would be pinned down in odd corners by uncles and aunts to be handed presents, and eventually everyone would gather together for a splendid tea which the children fairly tucked into, but for which the grownups seemed to have little appetite after a big Christmas lunch.

Beatrix's letters tell of how she and Willie joined this great family party after their marriage in 1913, and for several Christmases thereafter. Their usual present to other members of the family was a 'Hawkshead Cake', a round puff pastry tart like an Eccles cake, full of raisins and sugar. They also attended other occasions at Battlebarrow, including Blanche's funeral. Georgie Stampa's son, Arthur, remembered: 'I went back after the funeral to a good old Westmorland tea in the then seldom-used drawing room and helped dear Cousin May dispense. I remember taking the cakestand over to Beatrix who was sitting alone on the sofa. She said, "You don't know who I am". I replied: "I most certainly do, Cousin Beatrix". She looked at me with a wry smile and said, "Well done, Arthur".'

In a letter to a friend on the day that Willie was attending the funeral of his eldest brother, Alec (27 June 1925), Beatrix writes: 'He was the head of the family. He had been in bad health for nearly two years, but died suddenly, sitting in his chair [at Bongate Cross, Appleby]. He was a big, silent, responsible sort of man, courteous and very deaf. I had seen him three or four times when I was at Appleby, but scarcely knew him.'

Alec and his wife had given Willie and Beatrix a canteen of twelve settings of cutlery as a wedding present. Some years later on a rare visit to Sawrey from Appleby, Beatrix remarked to them, 'It was very nice of you to give us that canteen of cutlery, but half a dozen settings would have been quite enough.' Typical of Beatrix who liked to keep things simple and hated ostentation.

In another of her letters Beatrix mentions staying in Appleby for several days over Easter, '. . . which will freshen up my ideas'. And in yet another she praises the very good gardener at Battlebarrow, who was a Mr Burnell, and whose granddaughter still lives in the local Appleby area: 'The present Battlebarrow gardener is a treasure, keeping the lawns well mown, and the beds full of flowers.'

The old aunts always felt that the world revolved around Appleby, which to them was the hub of the universe. When the Stampa cousins

Alec as Mayor of Appleby.

Blanche and May in Battlebarrow garden.

wrote to them, they always asked what the latest news from the hub might be, and I continued this tradition when writing to Georgie's son, Arthur!

When I was a boarder at Appleby Grammar School in the 1930s I often used to slip in to visit Aunt May. She still used to make a wonderful brew of cider on an old press in the cellar. When my grandmother and I had tea with her, we usually found some excuse to send Aunt May off on an errand. As soon as she was out of the door my grandmother rushed to the coal bucket and put some more lumps on the fire – it was a cold house in the winter.

Aunt Blanche had always been very much the senior sister, and Aunt May was often a sad trial to her. My cousin, Ann Fearnhill, recalls that few mealtimes went by without May reaching across the table for something, which was always met with, 'Oh May! Why can't you ask?' May once sneezed at breakfast time. Blanche turned to Ann and explained, 'Your Aunt May has taken too much pepper.'

George and Willie at Battlebarrow House.

At a big family tea party in the summer, Ann remembers a huge bowl of strawberries and cream, so big that the serving spoons kept sliding into it and others had to be fetched. She remembers that six spoons disappeared into the bottom of the bowl. The day before this party Ann had had a very good tea and refused a piece of cake. This worried May, who tried her with apple pasty, biscuits and another kind of cake, but Ann had had enough to eat and declined them all. Suddenly, May exclaimed: 'I know what she'd like,' and set off for the door.

Blanche jumped to her feet and cried:

'May, I know what you're thinking and the answer's "no". It's for tomorrow.'

She followed her down the passage.

'Don't cut into it, May. No, May, not that.'

But it was too late. She had scooped out a big chunk from a beautifully moulded fruit jelly. Ann hopes she ate it, but at this distance of time she cannot remember.

The smells of China tea, kippers, box hedges and paraffin lamps and the sound of rooks cawing still bring Battlebarrow back vividly to Ann. Other memories include the unusual mushroomy smell of May's storeroom and the steel engravings on the stairs, including the fat boy, *Daniel Lambert, The Industrious Apprentice* and *The Late Scholar*. At the top of the house was a print room with pictures pasted on to the walls and on to a door leading through to the attic bedrooms for the maids. All this is sadly no more as the house was requisitioned by the army during the last war and the graffiti added by the soldiers were considered too rude by the George Heelises who succeeded to the property, and so were painted over.

Battlebarrow House was only a field away from Appleby Grammar School, very handy for the many Heelises who lodged in the house in term-time. A well-known headmaster in my father's day was Mr H.A.C. Counsell (nicknamed 'Hack'). One of his daughters Pat recalled,

I have many memories of Battlebarrow with Miss Blanche, of whom we were afraid, and Miss May, whom we liked, instinctively feeling that she was on a child's side. Old Mr Stampa used to sit with a black skull cap, looking at one with his fierce black eyes, though he was not as fierce as he looked. Lelio Stampa of course became a friend and later my tutor; I was in touch with him till he died. When we were children we used to go on long walks with him and our father. I also used to see a lot of Nancy [Nicholson] because, for a time, we had lessons together. I met her sisters Isabel and Esther too.

I do not remember ever meeting Willie Heelis, but I have a vivid memory of Beatrix Potter – sometime towards the end of the First World War. She had been visiting Battlebarrow and had walked along to the school drive. We three older children rushed out to meet the oncoming figure, but on getting nearer turned on our heels and fled at the sight of this extraordinary person in boots and weird clothes. Later we were summoned into the drawing room to meet her. She laughed and said 'You were frightened of me weren't you? Thought I was an old farmer's wife didn't you?' To which, not very diplomatically, we said yes.

I have a copy of *The Tale of Miss Moppett* and inside is written 'Pat Counsell, with love from Mrs W. Heelis, Christmas 1916'. Being a horribly precocious reader I was into Sax Rohmer by then and was furious at being given *Miss Moppett*. But the years have gone by and it is now, bound up with Sellotape, one of my most treasured possessions. As a toddler my eldest daughter demanded that it be read to her over and over again until she knew it by heart and more or less taught herself to read by it.

Nancy remembers having lessons with Pat Counsell at about the age of ten or eleven for the Common Entrance Exam. Gillian Counsell and Rosemary Heelis also attended. The teacher was the sister of P.F. Smith, a master at the grammar school. Nancy had to get up each morning at 6 o'clock, eat a bowl of porridge and then walk across the fields from their house, Ashton Lea, to Kirkby Thore railway station. Getting out at Appleby station with her books in a satchel on her back, she then walked to Battlebarrow with a carrier bag in her hand containing a can of fresh milk, and once a week a pound of butter, for her aunts. Having delivered the milk

Hawkshead Hall with the old courthouse in the foreground.

to Battlebarrow where her aunts and Uncle Stampa were having breakfast, Nancy went down the hill to Slapestone House for her lessons, returning to Battlebarrow for lunch; she considered Aunt Blanche a very good cook. Nancy returned to Kirkby Thore by train in the afternoon.

While she was still alive, Blanche kept strict control over the housekeeping money, but May was not to be outdone. She made a little kitchen on the top floor, which Blanche never visited, and cooked extra meals for herself on an oil stove. Blanche was somewhat retiring and did not go out much, but May had a pony and kept hens next door to the gardener's cottage on the other side of the road. She also kept rabbits for a time and dried off the skins in the top attics. She ran the local Red Cross Hospital in

Borwick Lodge, Hawkshead.

Appleby throughout the First World War and was awarded the MBE. She did a lot for the Girl Guides. Because Blanche liked to keep control of the flower garden and walled kitchen garden, May created a magical small garden of her own, entered through a doorway, very like one of Beatrix's illustrations. When she finally took charge herself she was getting old, and presented a sad figure all on her own in the big house which had seen so many of the family living there. Only memories remained to her.

Ann must be given the last world on Battlebarrow.

The last time I saw Aunt May she must have been about ninety. She led us out into the garden for a game of croquet. She was soon far ahead of everyone else and was at the last hoop. The sun was low, and the final post cast a long shadow under the hoop and on to the ball. Jokingly, I said, 'You only need to roll the ball along the shadow.' It was a very long shadow and looked impossible. 'That's right, dear,' May said, and duly hit the ball straight along the shadow to beat us all hollow!

CHAPTER FIVE

THE HAWKSHEAD HEELISES

W hen Willie Heelis moved from Appleby to join the Heelis solicitor's office in Hawkshead, the partners were William Hopes Heelis and his son William Dickenson Heelis. The firm was established in Hawkshead in 1836, the principals being John Raven and John Slater, with their office at what is still known as Slater's Yard. Subsequently an Edward Heelis joined the firm, thus providing a link with the Heelis family solicitor's connections in Appleby, Bolton, Manchester and London, and the firm was renamed Slater and Heelis. After Mr Slater's time it became W. and W.H. Heelis in Hawkshead and Ambleside. William Hopes Heelis was admitted a solicitor in 1854 and his son in 1888.

The Heelis office, Hawkshead.

Highfield, Hawkshead.

Our Willie Heelis, on taking up his office duties became known as Appleby Billy to distinguish him from William Dickenson who was known as Hawkshead Willie. He was admitted a solicitor in 1899, the same year as he joined. A number of people have speculated as to where he lived before marrying Beatrix and moving into Castle Cottage, Sawrey. The answer is that he lodged with William Dickenson's two spinster sisters, who lived firstly at Sandground and later moved to Hawkshead Hall. Their names were Frances Ann – always known within the family as Cousin Fanana – and Emily Jane. The two ladies lived on at Hawkshead Hall until they died in 1920 and 1931 respectively.

In 1900 William Hopes died and Willie became a partner with 'W.D.'. By a strange coincidence Willie had served his articles with a London and Hendon firm of solicitors called Potter and Co., but it should be noted that they had no connection with the lady he was subsequently to marry.

Esthwaite Mount.

For many years Willie was Clerk to the Justices at Hawkshead, Ambleside and Windermere. His nephew and partner, Jack Heelis, took over this task from him and continued until 1946 when he resigned due to pressure of work. Thus ended the holding of that appointment by four members of the Heelis family from the same firm over a period of ninety years. With that sort of background it was obvious that the Heelis office at Hawkshead was the place for Beatrix to go for advice when she started buying property and farms in the local area, and she valued the advice and help she was given very highly. Before she moved north permanently, Willie looked after her interests and kept her informed on how things were going in letters to London. When she came up on visits they often used to walk the property together, frequently on Sunday afternoons. Willie also used to visit her on his motor cycle in Sawrey when they had business to discuss. After they married she happily became Mrs Heelis, and quite often rebuked people who still insisted on calling her Miss Potter.

William Hopes Heelis's house in Hawkshead was Highfield, above the town on the road to Coniston. It is now a guest house. His wife, Augusta Sophia, died in 1899 and he died the year after. His son, W.D., together with his wife Sylvia Margaret, subsequently moved to Borwick Lodge, off the road to Tarn Hows. This too is now a guest house. They later moved for a short time to Croftlands above Colthouse on the road to Wray, and from there to the delightful house known as Esthwaite Mount. When W.D. died in 1930 he was in the process of having a house for his retirement built at Hannakin. His widow had it finished and lived there until her doctor forbade her to live alone any longer. She wanted to keep her independence and so moved into rooms at the King's Arms at Hawkshead where she remained till she died in 1946.

W.D.'s youngest sister, Dora Sophia, married Howard James Harrison, a relative of Harrison Ainsworth, the novelist. They lived at Yew Bank at Roger's Ground on the road to Grizedale. Mr Harrison used to terrify the local children who ventured too near the house through the woods by threatening them with a whip. When their daughter, Mabel Blanche Harrison, died in 1918 Yew Bank was bought by a Mr Hodgson for his

Presentation tea service from William Hopes Heelis to Edward Askew.

Timothy Askew's baker's cart from a contemporary photograph.

daughter. Mr Hodgson's maternal grandfather was Edward Askew who had been coachman to William Hopes Heelis for forty-three years until retiring in 1879, when he was given a plated tea service. His Uncle Timothy was the Timothy Baker in Beatrix's *Ginger and Pickles*, whose delivery van with his name on it appears in one of the illustrations. Edward Askew was nearly ninety years of age when he died. He was a well-known character in the Hawkshead area. He became a sergeant in the Hawkshead company of the 10th Lancashire Rifle Volunteers. He was the originator of a catch phrase coined for the Hawkshead company when he forgot the word of command that needed to be given and ordered the company to 'cludder up in t'back row'. On another occasion his patience as coachman was well-nigh exhausted waiting for Mrs Heelis, and he coolly informed her, 'Ye hev had a rare long chat!'

W.D.'s son, Leslie, educated at Appleby Grammar School, was destined to study law and join his father in the Hawkshead office. He was not keen on the idea and joined up in 1917, giving a false age. Beatrix writing to Grace Nicholson in February 1919 remarked: 'I was exceedingly amused to see Lesley [*sic*] yesterday

Timothy Askew's baker's cart as it appeared in *The Tale of Ginger and Pickles*. © Frederick Warne & Co., 1909, 1987.

riding a byke [*sic*] in spurs. He said the Army regulations did not permit him to take them off. I asked him if he went to bed in them! He also had a riding whip and a whistle which he blew loudly for the ferry without effect.' In the following December Leslie was still resisting studying law – Beatrix wrote to Grace 'I'm afraid the Hd [Hawkshead] family are at a complete loss what to do for Leslie, they say he wants to get something, but they seem very vague. Wm suggests curate! Rather rough on some future parish; how he would gas in a pulpit.' Leslie joined up again in the Second World War, leaving his wife and two daughters at Hawkshead. The daughters, Joan and Ann, remember Beatrix's weekly visits in a chauffeur-driven car to visit the bank. She always asked how they were when she saw them, and quite often had them over to tea at Sawrey. They remembered too how Beatrix made the Pekingese dogs, Tzusee and Chuleh, perform tricks, balancing sugar lumps on their noses and dancing around in circles.

They watched (at a distance!) Beatrix judging sheep at Hawkshead Show, and recalled how much she hated the hound trailing – in particular the amount of betting that went on. 'Mrs Heelis is creating about the betting again', they heard one official say.

Joan and Ann also visited Mrs W.D. (their grandmother) at the King's Arms, where her rooms consisted of a bedroom and her own sitting room, with a caged canary called Dickie, for which they brought raw carrot. She was most insistent on them being properly dressed, including long gloves. Their father, Leslie, was also ticked off one day for calling on her in

Yew Bank, home of Howard James Harrison.

battledress, which she did not consider a proper form of clothing for calling. They confirmed that Mrs W.D. did not approve of Beatrix, and that they seldom met. She probably did not approve of Beatrix's old black felt hat and clogs. After farming in both England and Ireland, where his first wife died, Leslie married again and moved to New Zealand, where he later died.

Leslie's sister, Sylvia, married George Ward Usher, whose parents had moved to Colthouse near Hawkshead. They spent some time in Ceylon, living on their return for some fifteen years in the Hawkshead area. Their old house in Hawkshead is now a pottery and houses have been built on what used to be their garden across the road. In their retirement the Ushers moved to the Isle of Man where George died. His widow lived on into her nineties in a nursing home in Ramsey. She died there in 1992.

The partner that Willie took into the Hawkshead office was Jack Heelis, the son of his brother, the Revd Thomas Heelis, Rector of Crosthwaite, whose wife, Ada Isabella, was also a Heelis from Bolton in Lancashire, thus linking the Bolton and Appleby branches of the family. Jack and his wife, Wynne, later became members of the Oxford Group, as did the Ushers, and they had prayer meetings at each other's houses on Tuesdays and Fridays. In a letter to Esther Nicholson, Beatrix says: 'They say it has made them much happier. Jack does not seem to come to the office any more punctually; but it is harmless. And where people are quarrelsome probably quite beneficial . . . I am not conscious of hating anybody; and your Uncle cannot publicly confess his sins as a solicitor nor other people's.'

Willie, Thomas (father of Jack and Hilary) and George.

Beatrix's hope that joining the Group might reduce quarrels was not altogether borne out. A feature of being 'groupy' (which was how Jack's brother, Hilary, described it) was to speak absolutely honestly, which led Wynne to say to Hilary's wife, Winnie (referring to her daughter), 'Ann's conversation does amuse me. She has your pompous way of expressing herself.'

Ann's mother was not one to let scores go unsettled, so a little later, when Wynne said, 'You'd never have thought that Jack would testify in public, would you?' Winnie replied: 'Since we're all being so truthful, Wynne, I can say that I would certainly have hoped not!'

Both of Jack and Wynne's children died in infancy, and sadly he himself was only forty-eight when he died in 1947, two years after his uncle.

Beatrix kindly allowed Jack and Wynne to live at Hill Top during the earliest part of their marriage until they could get a house of their own. She felt that they eventually rather outstayed their welcome and longed to get it

The Grassings, home of Willie's partner, Jack.

back for herself, the place where she could go and relax and write, surrounded by her own things. They eventually bought a very nice house, The Grassings, between Outgate and Hawkshead, below Belmount Hall. Wynne lived on there after Jack died until she herself died in 1973. She was a great flower arranger, and all her friends and colleagues transformed Hawkshead Church with flowers for her funeral.

Beatrix's cousin, Sir William Hyde-Parker, his wife Ulla, and children, William and Elizabeth, were the first people to live in Hill Top after Jack and his wife moved to The Grassings. In her book *Cousin Beatie*, Lady Hyde-Parker describes how much they enjoyed living there after leaving Melford Hall in Norfolk during the war when it was requisitioned by the Army, and after her husband had had a very serious operation as a result of an accident in the Home Guard in the blackout. Beatrix did not like other people going through her drawers and cupboards and was glad to have it back again after the war, but was of course delighted that she had been able to help her cousins out in this way. Beatrix was very worried when they had a Christmas tree with lighted candles, fearing that her beloved Hill Top and all her precious possessions were going to burn down.

A Mr William Powell, then aged eighty-eight, telephoned me in the summer of 1994 with his memory of the Heelis office at Hawkshead. As a District Valuer for the old counties of Cumberland and Westmorland, Mr Powell visited all the solicitors' offices in the area. He thus often visited Willie Heelis, who was a heavy smoker. He clearly remembered that when Willie finished smoking a cigarette he threw the stub into his office fireplace, which rarely seemed to be cleared out. Mr Powell swore that there were literally thousands of cigarette stubs in the fender.

Mrs Betty Ingham, the granddaughter of coachman Edward Askew, was only twenty-one and a new bride when she moved into Yew Bank, mentioned earlier. She and her husband, nine years older than herself, ran it as a guest house. At that time there was a finely carved wooden fireplace with the word 'PERSEVERANCE' carved on it by Sophie Harrison (née Heelis). Being somewhat nervous about her ability to run a guest house at such an early age, her father told her that it was a good motto for her to follow. The new owners removed the fireplace when the Inghams sold the house. Mrs Ingham's comment on the photograph of the Heelis office on page 32 was that she felt sure that the pony and trap in the foreground was standing nearby for her grandfather Edward Askew to take Mr W.H. Heelis back from his office to his house Highfield.

As a final footnote to this chapter, it is interesting to note that the Armitt sisters, who founded the Armitt Library and Museum at Ambleside, lived at Borwick Lodge for eight years in the 1880s and 1890s. W.D. Heelis had moved to Borwick Lodge from Highfield. Willie Heelis was a trustee of the Armitt Library for thirty years and Beatrix left to it many books and drawings, including her famous fungi drawings. Sophia Armitt's watercolour of Borwick Lodge is illustrated on page 21 of Warne's *A Victorian Naturalist – Beatrix Potter's Drawings from the Armitt Collection* (by Eileen Jay, Mary Noble and Anne Stevenson Hobbs), and on p. 24 of that book there is a pen and wash drawing of Pillar House, Hawkshead, in 1886. This was the house where Mrs Edward Askew lived in her old age.

CHAPTER SIX

TEA WITH AUNT BEATRIX

Jack Heelis's brother, Hilary Loraine, a partner in the firm of Broadbent and Heelis of Bolton, died in 1938, leaving a daughter, Ann Loraine, who gave us some of her memories of Appleby in Chapter Four. Ann also remembers going to tea with her Great Aunt Beatrix at Castle Cottage, Sawrey in the 1930s. She was looking forward to the typical tea provided in most houses in those days – brown and white bread-and-butter, scones, jam, pastries and cakes. As a well-brought-up little girl Ann knew that she must eat up her bread-and-butter before going on to cakes and biscuits. At Castle Cottage there was no dainty, ready buttered bread on a plate, just a loaf of bread with butter to spread on it. She remembers it was on a table covered with a green tablecloth with bobbles hanging down from it. Ann did justice to the rather hearty bread-and-butter in the hope of better things to come, so she kept nudging her mother for the cake that she hoped might follow. Her mother kicked her under the table – surreptitiously she hoped – but Beatrix turned to her and said, 'If the child's still hungry, there's plenty more bread – she'll get nothing else in this house.' Ann also remembers going for a walk with her aunt, who told her about the wild flowers and birds and animals they saw. They were accompanied by the Pekingese dogs, Tzusee and Chuleh. Beatrix's comment to Ann when Ann asked the name of a plant was, 'It's called Enchanter's Nightshade. It isn't a nightshade and it isn't at all enchanting, but apart from that I suppose it's quite a good name.'

Ann recalls how her father, who owned a bull mastiff, and her Uncle Jack, who had cocker spaniels, had nothing but scorn for Beatrix's Pekingese, until one November morning they got out and killed nine turkeys, which cost Uncle Willie the then vast sum of £9. The brothers came to the conclusion that Tzusee and Chuleh weren't Pekes at all, but quite decent little sporting dogs.

Sylvie Heelis.

Castle Cottage from the front garden today.

When rather older, Ann wrote a story for the *Mickey Mouse Weekly* which was accepted. Her proud mother, Winnie, sent Beatrix a copy. Beatrix took the trouble to send her a very good critique on it afterwards, which has unfortunately been destroyed. We can, however, read her comments on an unpublished story by my Aunt Sylvie Heelis, the daughter of Willie's brother, Alec, in Judy Taylor's 'Letters' book. Sylvie's story was called 'Prickuls', concerning a teasel, about which Beatrix wrote: 'I should not (candidly) have chosen a teasle [*sic*] for a hero myself.' The original letter is in my possession. Sylvie also wrote quite good poems and Beatrix encouraged her to write more. Beatrix's kindness and patience in encouraging the literary efforts of her nieces was typical. It belies the often-heard suggestion that she disliked children.

45

Ap. 16. 37

Castle Cottage
Sawrey
Ambleside

My dear Sylvie,

I am as slow as a publisher, I am very sorry! though the return of the mss. herewith does not include condemnation. I like them. I am afraid poetry is turned out by the mile. Have you ever tried to get into print? If you have a wish that way you might send half a dozen (not, I think, more) to "Country Life" 20 Tavistock Street Strand WC2. The successive editors have always had a pleasant taste in poetry, 2 poems weekly, for a many years, The paper has published poems by writers who have re published in book form & succeeded into fame later!! Also the pleasant country lyrics of unknown country lovers - never heard of again; I have often cut them out. Luckily the writer experiences the pleasure of composition even if the effort gets no further. I tried to help a friend with a novel last winter, she said I had been helpful; but still it came back. Very difficult to judge. Even publishers makes make mistakes. "The Hiring" "The Moth", have a Country Life appeal. (Only plops is rather bitten.?) "What odds the fell?

First page of a letter from Beatrix to Sylvie Heelis
commenting on her poems.

46

very good, and pretty in small compass.
You get a word not quite happy at times. "freedom" is let down
by the last line. "fluidity" reminds of oil immersion a fluid
moving wheel – perhaps you meant it – but it jars. "Sonnet"
very good. drawback – not entirely original in thought.
What then shall curb the living soul – . shall? must?
please find a better word than "fluidity". "If this be love –
very ... pleasing echoes of Herrick. not irreverence – (I
thought of C.L. ... 'Matches matches' this has been done so
often; imitating Kipling?? it does need to be extra clever to ...
I never guessed you were a poet, though I thought you were ...
a philosopher, with awareness of the problems of life, masked ...
jerky manner! The poetry is not to be ashamed of, or shy about
excepting so far as delicate pretty thoughts accord with retirement.
I have not exhibited them to the probably brutal comments of
your uncle Willy who would not be likely to understand
them & I have read them with complete understanding and
pleasure; and I am glad with you and for you that you
have a soul; and "seeing-eye-of-memory" for the red ploughland
of the north and the curlews crying, to help keep the soul
alive in the racket and roar of London which in spite of its
fluidity, its spinning racing pace, is still drab and a bit
sordid. I used to think the least drab, the most genuinely
alive side of London was in the east-end and working class
London – fifty sixty years ago, at any rate it was just like Dickens
(whom I cannot now read). I was not well before Easter, but I am
alright again. I have been very busy which is my excuse for delay.
With love yr aff. Aunt Beatrix.

Second page of the letter from Beatrix to Sylvie Heelis
commenting on her poems.

Two of Sylvie's poems mentioned in the letter are as follows:

THE HIRINGS

Come Michaelmas Fair in the market I'll stand,
With a straw in my mouth and a straw in my hand.
And if farmer don't hire me the bigger fool he,
For a better-working lad never could be.

And when I've some brass, then to parson I'll go
And take out a licence, and let the folks know
That the bonniest lass in the whole countryside
Is yourself, lovely Mary, my sweetheart – my bride.

THE NORTH

Tell me, what of the North?
Are the fields ploughed red for the sowing?
Do plovers cry as the shares go by,
And is the helm-wind blowing?

Does Flakebridge stand where it stood,
With its sombre pine-trees swaying?
Do pheasants strut near the keeper's hut,
And are the rabbits playing?

That Eden runs where she ran
Is sure as the age-old story;
While tier upon tier, the Pennines rear
Vast sinuous limbs in glory.

Oh! Tell me, what of the North?
Are the sun and the rain-clouds flying?
Do the larks still sing? Does the silence ring
With the curlew's haunted crying?

On the subject of meals at Castle Cottage, I was told by Mrs Macon of Outgate how a friend had been invited to lunch with Beatrix before they both went off to a local furniture sale. This consisted of a quick clearance of papers and writing materials from half the dining room table and then sitting down to a plate of cold mutton on the other half. Mrs Macon was the daughter of Major Boddington, who had served in the Boer War, the First World War, where he was gassed, and the Second World War. He was a good shot and liked shooting with Willie.

Mrs Mollie Green (née Byers) who served home-made teas to visitors to Sawrey at her home, Anvil Cottage, each summer, told me that her mother had a bakery and confectioner's shop there. Every Friday they baked pork pies and Beatrix came regularly to pick up a fresh pie to take back to Castle Cottage. She also told me that her mother used to sell Hawkshead cake, but not the big round ones that Beatrix and Willie sent as Christmas presents. Mollie gave me another instance of Beatrix's kindness and consideration. Mollie's mother was dying and in pain, which increased every time one of the heavy wood lorries thundered past the house to the sawmill. Beatrix heard of this and arranged that the lorries should stop going for a while, making Mrs Byers' last days easier for her.

CHAPTER SEVEN

DID BEATRIX REALLY DISLIKE CHILDREN?

Ann Fearnhill (née Heelis), the same Ann who had tea with Beatrix in the last chapter, certainly did not think that Beatrix disliked children when she read some disparaging remarks on the subject by the late Roald Dahl in a Sunday newspaper not long ago. Her letter to the editor which followed summed up the feelings of most of us in the family, and many others as well:

> I would like to protest most strongly against Roald Dahl's silly, uninformed comment about my Great Aunt Beatrix Potter (Mrs William Heelis), stating that she 'hated children' and 'when she saw one coming . . . she used to throw stones at it'.
>
> During my childhood I had tea with Aunt Beatrix about four times a year. I don't think she liked me particularly because I don't think I was a very likeable child, and she was far too intelligent and discriminating to 'love' people for no better reason than they were children. She certainly showed affection and friendship to other children in the family, and to individual children for whom many of her books were written, and was pleasant and forbearing to me. She was an independent and outspoken lady (I use the term 'lady' deliberately), but she was also well-bred and sane, and the idea of her throwing a stone for any other reason than to play ducks and drakes is ludicrous.

In contrast to Ann Fearnhill's opinion is the comment of Beatrix's tenant farmer at Hill Top, Tom Storey, whom she trusted so implicitly that she chose him to scatter her ashes on her land and tell no one where he had done so. Some years after her death, in a television commentary, Tom said, 'I don't think she liked children.' Amanda Thistlethwaite, the daughter of Possy Postlethwaite, Beatrix's neighbour at High Green Gate Farm in Sawrey, who was Farmer Potatoes in the *Tale of Samuel Whiskers*, also said that she was scared of her. At the same time she acknowledged that she might have been rude to her at times, so perhaps it was deserved. She may just have been following her father's example as he and Beatrix had many an argument over the years. Amanda's mother used to tell Possy not to argue so much as he was usually in the wrong, but he said he was not going

Ann with Winnie and Hilary at Hill Top.

to let Beatrix boss him like she bossed everyone else in the village. Beatrix usually just stomped off at the end of each session. She probably felt it sharpened her wits a bit. She certainly used to listen in to some of Possy's conversations with his friends, and she used these as chats between the dogs in *The Fairy Caravan*. A conversation between Fan and Mettle runs as follows: 'Does Mistress Heelis ever take her clogs off? In fact I thought she went to bed in them!'

Tommy Christopherson, who worked for the Heelises on the farm during the Second World War, and later took over from Walter Stevens as their chauffeur, was also said to be outspoken to the point of rudeness, but again Beatrix apparently just used to shrug it off. I think she rather enjoyed an argument.

Mrs Rogerson, the housekeeper at Castle Cottage, found Beatrix very quiet and secretive at times. When she was engrossed in her writing she would hardly speak for days. When she saw her for the first time in the morning, Mrs Rogerson could always tell whether it was wise to speak to her or not. Yet she was so often just the opposite, very nice, and doubly so when she heard of someone in real need. Mrs Rogerson went so far as to say that she only remembered one child that Beatrix really took to, and that she seemed to have difficulty in striking a warm contact with children.

I tackled Amanda as to whether she was really being fair when, in an interview on television with Hunter Davies, she said that Beatrix had been mean in only giving £2 as a wedding present when she married Mr Thistlethwaite. Amanda had told Hunter Davies how Beatrix had come to the house saying, 'Mr Heelis tells me I must get you a wedding present', and was taken in to see the presents they had been given. She grunted and said, 'You've got everything', and wrote out the cheque. In fact it was quite a lot of money in those days, but Amanda felt it was not as generous as another cheque they had been given, or a rather fine eiderdown given by another friend. Amanda rather gave the show away, however, when she confided to me that she wished she had kept the cheque for the signature rather than cashing it!

My own personal memory of my Great Aunt Beatrix was a visit as a young boy with my parents. I remember that she was wearing clogs, had a sack tied round her middle, and that the kitchen at Castle Cottage had a flagged floor. She took me on a tour of Hill Top, which I much enjoyed. I did not find her anti-child. I thought her kind and gentle, though a bit eccentric, and other relatives agree.

My mother never really forgave her for nearly kidnapping me from my prep school. I told the story to Judy Taylor who used it in her book, but it is worth telling again. I was at my school, Charney Hull, Grange-over-Sands, when my father died suddenly in 1933, aged only forty-two. I shall never forget the headmaster, Conrad Podmore, gathering the whole school together but taking me on one side. Exactly the same thing had happened the year before to another boy whose father had died so I sensed and feared that something dreadful had happened in my family even before the news was gently broken to me. The next week Aunt Beatrix arrived in her car at the school, knocked on the door and asked to see the headmaster. She knew we had been left very badly off, and announced that my trunk was to be

David and John Heelis as boys in Appleby.

packed immediately and that she would take me off then and there to The Craig at Windermere. Beatrix and Willie knew the headmaster at this school, which Willie's godson, Colin Heelis, had attended.

Conrad Podmore reacted quickly. He sent me off, without me knowing the reason, on a long walk into the countryside with the matron, Miss Hodgson, while his wife rang my mother to find out if she knew anything about it or had been consulted. She had not, of course, and was naturally upset. As it happened my fees had been paid for another term in advance, so there was no question of changing schools so suddenly. Beatrix had meant well, and it was a generous gesture, but her action in this instance at least was not appreciated by my mother.

Subsequently Willie and Beatrix took over the payment of my brother David's education at a prep school in the South of England, and later at Taunton School, while Willie's brother, George, paid for my education at Appleby Grammar School and later Bedford School before I went on to Sandhurst.

Willow Taylor, another Sawrey near-neighbour of the Heelises, also said that she was afraid of Beatrix. She recalled that Sawrey village school had two classrooms, two teachers and forty-eight children on the school roll. The children had the freedom of the local woods and fields, but must never be seen on Mrs Heelis's land otherwise they were in trouble. Unfortunately Willow always seemed to be getting caught while retrieving balls from the Post Office meadow. During the war, when chocolate was either not available or severely rationed, Beatrix used to receive parcels from overseas sometimes containing chocolate. Willow could not help feeling envious when she saw Beatrix feeding chocolates to the Pekingese dogs without offering any to the children. Not perhaps unkind, but a bit unthinking.

And yet I have heard how much the Sawrey children enjoyed the parties given for them by Willie and Beatrix each year. The furniture in the long parlour was either moved right out, or back by the walls. Willie would play the pianola, and the party always started with everyone dancing the 'Sir Roger de Coverley', followed by other traditional country dances such as 'The Squirrel'. Other games would include 'Hunt the Thimble' and a treasure hunt. Willie would demonstrate some country dances and enjoyed joining in the dancing. Amanda told me that Willie and Beatrix also used to get the children together during the war to collect foxglove leaves, which were used to extract digitalin, a heart stimulant.

Dennis Benson, one of the children of Beatrix's tenant at Troutbeck Park Farm, disagreed with those who claimed that Beatrix disliked children. They were each given a book by Beatrix every Christmas. 'Yes we had to touch our forelock to her as taught by our parents, but that was normal in those days.' One year they had a young cousin, Henry, staying with them. Beatrix was embarrassed when she came with the other children's books that she had nothing for him. As soon as she returned to Sawrey she wrote a letter to Henry enclosing money for a present.

Anyone who disliked children would surely not have welcomed Girl Guides and Boy Scouts to camp on her land as Beatrix did. She also showed her concern for them by letting them move into one of her barns when the weather was very wet. She enjoyed attending their camp fires and even lent her car and chauffeur to drive a girl with suspected appendicitis to hospital. The villagers may have been scared of her, but they knew that she had their welfare at heart, even if they did not necessarily want what she was doing for them! They surely must have approved of her generosity in buying all the dresses for a folk dance festival in Sawrey during the country and folk dance craze after the Second World War.

'Certainly she was crusty at times, but within the crust the heart was sound', was the writer J.H.B. Peel's opinion. Every year she designed cards for the Invalid Children's Aid Association. Any tramp that called at Castle Cottage would receive a shilling, a cup of tea and a piece of cake. The carol singers at Christmas were given hospitality and tipped when they called at the house. Rather than saying that she disliked children, might it not be fairer to say that she detested excessive noise, and became increasingly disenchanted with the hordes of visitors and children who began to visit Sawrey, even in her lifetime, and especially when they peered into her garden and even followed her down the street?

Josephine Banner told me that she felt really angry when she heard the frequent comments that Beatrix disliked children. Beatrix told her that she had to be strict with the Sawrey children otherwise they took advantage of her, invading the privacy of her house and garden. She took children who wanted news of 'Peter Rabbit' into her garden where she always had two rabbits in a wired-in box on the lawn, moved each day to give them fresh grass and act as a mobile mowing machine. She said to Josephine: 'I always have to keep some rabbits, as children who visit me expect to meet Peter Rabbit. I don't think I'm being too dishonest when I tell them they are direct relations of the original Peter.'

'The last time I saw Beatrix was in the Castle Cottage garden,' Josephine told me. 'We both knew it was our last meeting, and typical of us both, we said nothing. She put out her chubby little hands and pulled down my face – and kissed me. It was a quiet summer afternoon, and my way out was soundless across the grass . . . I turned and saw her standing in the gateway waving a clover leaf and looking just like Timmy Willy. To me she was understanding and caring – to her I was "Dear Pigwig".'

I do not think that Beatrix really disliked children, but she liked them to be well behaved. The fact that the village children were scared of her was surely partly due to her odd dress and her habit of walking with her head down, and also to the fact that she had the guts to tick them off if she felt that they were being cheeky, too forward, were acting immorally or were simply behaving badly. In a letter to Joe Moscrop in 1940, Beatrix remarks: 'When I see a parcel of lads loafing at a corner on a Sabbath afternoon – I wonder whether they would not be better on the recreation ground instead of idling and shouting bawdy talk to get rid of their superfluous energy?' She would not have liked many of the spoilt children of today who are rarely disciplined by their parents and so often turn into drop-outs or vandals. Who can say that she would not have been right?

She appreciated that children traditionally enjoyed taking apples from orchards, but she did not see why they should always take her best ones. She therefore put a ribbon round the trees they could help themselves from but woe betide anyone caught raiding any of the others! She was perhaps somewhat insensitive to other people's feelings and did not always understand the ways of children, but I am sure she did not dislike them.

I think that a letter from Mrs M.R. Ormerod of Reading in the *Radio Times* of 13 May 1971 says it all:

We went to live in Sawrey in 1919, and after about a year Beatrix Potter came to see me to ask if I would employ a Sawrey girl in whom she was interested. This I was glad to do, and after that she invited our elder son, aged six, and me to tea in her cottage. He was well read in her books, and they got on very well together. I remember that he asked her if she would write a story about our goats, but she said that she would write no more stories as her eyesight was not good enough for her to do the illustrations. She gave our children two delightful hard-boiled Easter eggs painted by herself – one showed the head of a child with golden curls and blue eyes, and the other the head of an old man with a bald head and side whiskers. I kept the eggs for many years in a display cabinet.

When we regretfully had to leave Sawrey to live in a town she kindly volunteered to take over our children's pet rabbits. They had a great deal of freedom with us, and we were afraid that a new owner might shut them in boxes.

Beatrix Potter was eccentric, but if one respected her idiosyncrasies and her desire for privacy she was friendly and kind. I have very happy memories of my meetings with her.

Beatrix's famous early picture letters to 'Noel' were not written by someone who disliked children. She had still not lost her touch or understanding of what a child would be interested in when she wrote the following to Nancy Nicholson, who was sick in bed, in November 1919.

I have two new pigs called Peggy and Biddy, very nice little pigs, especially Biddy. I always feed her out of the bucket because Peggy is strongest and gets it all if they both go to the trough. I still have Sarah, I am stuffing her. She is enormous, also her appetite is wheelbarrowfuls. I am a little tired of her to tell the truth; she is not bad tempered, but for some time past she has been getting a little pig headed . . . Dolly [pony], is very well, she had been nosing about in the snow. I wonder whether that is why mountain ponies have such beards! It answers for a snow brush anyway. I have got a white drake called Mr Sykes. He has a mind to get himself killed; he goes for the turkey hens, he objects to them feeding with his duck ladies. He stands on his toes and pulls out mouthfuls of feathers, and when I get one hen away he attacks the other. After he had been knocked down twice and pecked through the head I shut him up. I shall have to keep him in a different place, perhaps inside the garden. The ducks are most admiring and interested in these fights, and when Mr Sykes is in a hen coup they go and talk to him, tremendous quack quacks. I heard them second day after he arrived, I was in the house, I peeped over the wall, there was [sic] 4 ducks showing Mr Sykes the Oakmen's hollow tree, they were all talking at once standing in front of the hole. I shall know where to look for ducks eggs. That tiny kitten, which Judy picked up is still here. It has been rather near an 'accident' several times! I don't like kittens that get under the fire grates. At one time it drove us nearly wild with going up our stockings, especially Uncle Willie, it usually fell off when it got to the garters, then it rushed up the other leg, it made him mad. Ribby [cat] is very rough with it, but it does not care. Ribby is very fluffy, and will be a good mouser. Judy [cat] has a cold in one eye. Fleet [sheep dog] is very well.

That was not written by someone who disliked children.

CHAPTER EIGHT

MRS HEELIS, FARMER

After marriage Beatrix concentrated much more on farming and on acquiring buildings and land for conservation than on writing. Her only publications were *Pigling Bland* in the year of her marriage, followed by *Appley Dapply's Nursery Rhymes*, *Johnny Town-Mouse*, *Cecily Pursley's Nursery Rhymes*, *Little Pig Robinson*, *The Fairy Caravan* and a few others published originally only in America.

She had been busy for some years with the farm at Hill Top in conjunction with John Cannon and his wife, and had enlarged the farmhouse to give separate accommodation for herself at one end, and for the Cannons at the other. They had gradually expanded their flock of sheep and there were hens, ducks, turkeys, and collies for rounding up the sheep including her favourite, Kep, cows and a bull, and pedigree pigs. Since 1903 she had also taken possession of Castle Cottage Farm, with Mrs Rogerson looking after the cottage as housekeeper. In 1913 she was busy preparing Castle Cottage for herself and Willie to live in. She improved and expanded it, but continued to use Hill Top as her library and for spare rooms.

Somehow over the earlier years of farming she had managed to continue to supply Frederick Warne and Co. with new titles for publication, many of them including sketches of her farm animals and poultry, and scenes around Hill Top Farm and Sawrey village. But now with a husband to look after, her mother to keep an eye on after she moved north from London, and the added difficulties of farming caused by the First World War with men called up, she just couldn't continue to produce her 'little books' regularly any more, though she was under constant pressure to do so.

In 1916 Beatrix employed a Miss Eleanor L. Choyce (known to her friends as Louie), and her brother Tom, to help with the farming. Beatrix told Miss Choyce in the letter she wrote to her explaining what the job entailed, that although she was very active and cheerful, she and the housekeeper were becoming very overworked. She explained that she and Willie lived very

An illustration from *The Tale of Jemima Puddle-Duck*. © Frederick Warne & Co., 1908, 1987.

quietly. Beatrix listed the duties of the Cannon family: John Cannon, cowman, foreman and shepherd; Mrs Cannon, dairy woman and farm housekeeper; and Willie Cannon, ploughman. She explained that she managed most of the cooking herself with the help of one young servant, and also the poultry, the orchard and the flower and vegetable garden; that she also often helped with the hay, and she 'singled' the turnips when she had the time.

Miss Choyce and her brother stayed at Hill Top, Beatrix making it clear that they must be careful tenants because the furniture and old oak was too good to be spoiled. They obviously all got on well together, as Beatrix continued to correspond with Miss Choyce for many years afterwards. In a letter dated 19 September 1922 Beatrix gives her an excellent description of her farming activities, and what a very active part she took herself:

. . . This season has been a nightmare, I shall always look back to it with a memory of . . . rushing in loads of corn in a gale of wind, with small rain coming in from the sea and ending in a pelt. We have only had one fine spell, Monday Sept 4th to Sept 11th since you left. Four days of it were hot, and we got in 2 fields of hay and the ley corn without a drop of rain. And John Taylor and I rushed some of the remaining corn into a little stack under a cart sheet. We have only a cart or two of hay still out, we got the clover corn yesterday under very nervous conditions, ending in a downpour which is still continuing. We were a fortnight in the post office meadow; except during the dry week we have had to cut little bits, and work it over and over. But we have had very little damaged by dint of hard work. Four carts of clover were very bad; they had been in cock a month. I salted the mow, I expect it will cut with the oats, which are excellent. All crops are a bit short. I shall have to sell some cattle. Was it after you left, the heifer hanged herself at Hawkshead Field? fell over a bank with its hind foot in a rabbit hole under a tree root. I have a nice family of little pigs arrived last Wednesday night (torrents of rain), as a rule the nights have been clear and cold; I think the extreme coldness of the earth has caused our bad weather. It has often been fine at Kendal, when we were in sea fog . . .

The hens are beginning to lay alright again, no pullet eggs yet, they were hatched rather late. The 9 big turkey chicks are fine birds; there were a lot of nests hatched out in July, turkeys and chickens all over the place, but all have died except 5 – over 30. Last summer I did not lose one of the late hatched . . . There is a great quantity of fruit, small and unripe, and much falling off, I shall now turn my mind upon apple and blackberry jelly.

In December of the same year Beatrix tells Miss Choyce:

I hope this Christmas I have the gratification of sorting out my turkeys, there are not enough to go round the customers. I lost such a lot of the July hatched. Your hens have done remarkably well, eggs have been very scarce; and saleable at 4/6 per dozen if anybody has had any to sell . . . I haven't heard just lately from Mrs Cannon, no doubt I will do so at Christmas when I send her a couple of rabbits. The men are trapping such fat ones.

She goes on to reveal her butcher activities:

If you please I am a BUTCHER! We have been butching on the quiet for a long time, and someone reported (one of the professional butchers as a matter of fact). He did nobody any harm but himself. We had always been careful to kill in the open air. The Council have now licensed the hall next the washhouse at Hill Top. We find that a sheep or lamb home killed makes about 20/- more than the market price and we can sell good meat for less than the butcher after all. Which the Council approve of; for once showing a little common sense.

In May 1923 Beatrix gives Miss Choyce news of a hen that had obviously been a favourite of hers: 'I forgot to give you news of Fenella when I wrote; she clucked but she did not sit! I think she is laying again, I brought her over here [Castle Cottage] when the Hill Top garden was planted with potatoes, so she is promenading with that Campine cockerel, I fancy they agree better, the hens treat her with respect.'

Two months later Beatrix gives further news of Fenella: '. . . I can't give Fenella a good summer character, I don't think she has laid 10 eggs since you left, continually clucking without sitting – at last I got her on to two eggs near hatching, but she has not much idea – Probably she will lay well in winter . . .'.

There were some tricky lambing seasons, more bad weather and difficult harvests to contend with, and then in 1918 Willie received his call-up papers, and Beatrix's brother Bertram died at the early age of forty-six. Mercifully Willie failed his medical and did not have to go, but it took her some time to get over Bertram's death. She and Willie had visited him and his wife nearly every summer for many years, and she had always been very close to him in early life.

After 1918 Willie's and Beatrix's life was rather less worrying, and Willie was able to go to his country dancing again, often proudly watched by Beatrix. In addition to her cows, sheep, horses and poultry she had become enthusiastic about breeding rabbits. She put more and more energy into her farming activities, culminating in the purchase in 1924 of the 2,000-acre Troutbeck Park Farm, which she visited regularly in a newly acquired Morris Cowley car, driven by Tommy Christie, a forester, who lived at Colthouse. Willie dealt with all the farming paperwork. After searching for just the right man, she employed Tom Storey to manage the new farm, and they became firm friends.

Before she arrived unannounced at the farm where Tom was working – he was just completing the hand-milking of a dozen Dairy Shorthorns – to ask him if he would work for her, she had gone round the district asking a number of her old farmer friends what sort of a man he was. He was just thirty at the time, married with two children. She was quite straightforward and asked him how much he was getting in wages. She offered him double and he accepted. That was on a Saturday, and he started work at Troutbeck Park on the Monday! Tom had always wanted to be a sheepman and his previous employer was moving to another farm and quite prepared to let him go.

Tom worked at Troutbeck Park for three years. He put rams to a thousand breeding ewes, and lambed them the following spring. He got 992 lambs marked out. Some not marked out were taken by the foxes. Up to that time lambing at Troutbeck Park had not been very good as it had a bad reputation for sheep fluke. Luckily a new cure came just at that time from a veterinary firm in Newcastle. It proved a great success.

Willie, although always busy at the office, found time to help with the hay, and sometimes proved useful in other ways, as when: '. . . a wasp got inside everything, and must have made William lively for once, he asserted himself on the hens and put down Mr Simpson to the satisfaction of J. Cannon!' On another occasion Beatrix wrote: 'Wm is very overworked – office is getting too much for him, but what can be done?'

Her old shepherd, Joseph Moscrop, often came back to help with the lambing. Beatrix felt that without him and his dog it wouldn't be like lambing time. They sold suckler calves at Harrison's and Hetherington's Auction Mart at Carlisle, but kept some back and sold them rather better at Penrith. She also sold two little black bulls locally for 10 guineas and 8 guineas. The top price obtained for her bullocks was £9 2s 6d.

In 1927 Beatrix moved Tom Storey from Troutbeck Park to Hill Top as she wanted him to help her breed and show good Herdwick sheep at the local agricultural shows. Knowing that Beatrix was very firm with her men at Hill Top, Tom had insisted that he must be the manager. She accepted this. The motor lorry used for heavy farm jobs brought all Tom's belongings down to Sawrey and he and his family settled in to the extension at Hill Top. Tom liked the large dairy which was cool as it did not get the sun. There was a separator for the milk used for producing butter and cheese. The cows were Shorthorns. Every morning Tom took one or two pints of milk over to Castle Cottage in a can in a basket. Beatrix always met him at the door. He would let her know how things were going at the farm.

Earlier on, Beatrix had argued with Tom about whether some of her sheep were fit to be shown. Tom held his ground and told her that if she wanted that particular batch showing she had better get her old shepherd, Mackereth, back again, Beatrix stumped off into Mrs Storey's kitchen at Hill Top saying that her husband was 'a bad-tempered little devil,' but once they had the measure of each other they got on very well together.

Beatrix liked the old ways and did not buy many items of modern machinery. She had a lot of hand implements, horses and carts, and a double-horse mowing machine. The Heelises were the last people in the village to have electricity put in, two years after it first arrived. When it first came Beatrix had it put in the shippon as she thought the cows might like it, but it went right past the farmhouse. She did not like the telephone, but used the public one at the Post Office to check up on how her mother was getting on.

Beatrix wrote to Miss Choyce in 1934:

My flock has taken a great many prizes at the local shows – over forty this summer, mainly for female sheep. But I have had to give back the champion cup; a young farmer from Grasmere has *one* ewe which beats my younger ewes, though I regularly beat him with a pair. Our old 'Waterlily' is still alive and has reared another prize winning lamb; but I insisted on retiring her last year, as I could see she was embarrassing to the judges! still the best sheep; but too ancient. She has bred a family of over a dozen descendants, all show specimens.

Sheep prices were better that year too and earlier in the same letter she wrote: 'My halfbred lambs averaged over £1 per head, top price 26/- . . . But Herdwick wool sticks at 4d. and I doubt if it will ever rise much because its main use was for making carpets – now everyone has parquet or linoleum . . . It cannot be helped. The poor sheep have to be clipped in summer.'

Beatrix was very thrifty. A story is told in the family that she was driven out one day to settle a bill she had with a local farmer. She met him at the end of his farm lane, and paid him there to save the ride up to the farmhouse. He had no money on him, so she waited at the end of the lane for some ten minutes while he walked back to the house to bring her a penny change!

Beatrix and Willie had a successful hatch of ducklings in the orchard opposite The Castle (the building next door to Castle Cottage), but they were so wild that they could not catch them. In the end Willie had to shoot the drake.

During the Second World War Beatrix and Willie experienced many of the farming difficulties they had had in the First World War. Miss Choyce returned to Sawrey to help them out. Beatrix worked very hard herself, but suffered now more and more from ill-health. Willie still helped all he could, but he was again short-handed at the office, and he too wasn't always very well: 'I wish Mr Heelis would get right, he has not been good this winter. I think there is a sort of flue [sic] that gets hold.' Willie rested when he could after helping on the farm. Beatrix wrote to Nancy in June 1932, 'Your Uncle is sleeping peacefully after assisting to put a mustard plaster on a cow.'

Joseph Moscrop continued to come back to help out with lambing and the clipping. Beatrix was always very fond of Joe, though she used to haggle over the amount he was paid. She wrote chatty and affectionate letters to him, such as this one from 1927: 'I can match your name-sake's coat of many colours . . . there is a *yellow* calf today!'

In 1934 she looked forward to his coming with the remark: 'You will be as welcome as the flowers of spring.' In 1940 she wrote to thank him for some toffees he had sent. One of her last letters, written in pencil with difficulty nine days before she died in December 1943, was to Joe, her favourite shepherd. She had not been well that summer, and had to spend more time indoors, but she kept in touch with everything that went on and was proud of the fact that they had had a very big crop of hay.

Another correspondence she obviously enjoyed was with Mr C.S. Forrester of Skitby, north of Carlisle on the border with Scotland. In a letter dated 13 January 1941 she said:

Will it be possible to buy a young galloway bull? . . . I hope I have not left the purchase too late for sales? . . . The white Dodd bull is still going strong, he is a beautiful beast . . . I think the war is turning to victory, but there will be much suffering yet – We can see the sky lighted up over the Lancashire towns. And we are rather near the Cumberland coast – I wonder where the invasion will be attempted?

Sheep farming has been ups and downs – lamb sales (stores) very disappointing . . . I fear a good many ewes were butchered that ought not to have been killed . . . I did well with the Herdwick wool . . . it made over two hundred pounds; and I remember selling for as little as £80 one season . . . Considering there is a war on – I don't think farmers are profiteering – do you? With increased costs there is not much margin. But it's very interesting!

She then goes on to discuss silage – a new development at that time: 'I wonder if you have tried silage. We find it invaluable. Some people who have bought cheap wire silos are having some waste . . . I bought a portable wooden silo £20 from Messrs English Bros, Wisbeach [*sic*]. I really think the stuff is almost better than cake . . . My husband and I keep well . . .'.

On 22 February 1941 she wrote glowingly about the bull Mr Forrester had sent: 'He is a beauty – so compact, which is what is required here – as some bred galloways grow too big . . . I think he is a particularly nice bull; we cannot find a fault'.

She wrote again in March 1941 still full of praise for the bull, which she said would be 'quite at home on the fells'. She went on to describe how she had watched a fight between two bulls: '. . . the little galloway knelt down and pummelled the white one from beneath under the ribs; the shorthorn would not fight, the herdman called the cows and the galloway remained in possession of the pasture . . .'.

On 11 March 1943 she wrote again to Mr Forrester saying that they proposed to collect a young bull he had got for her in a lorry she was sending from Hawkshead. She had had a touch of flu 'but soon got over it'. In June 1943 Beatrix told Mr Forrester. 'We kept one bullock . . . but it proved very cross while only a calf – ran at anybody going into the loose box – so he had to become beef . . .'.

She later went on to tell him about her meeting with Mr Hudson, the Minister of Agriculture.

I had an interesting experience meeting Mr Hudson though it was a wash-out – a fiasco! The telephone message said nothing about *cattle*, I thought it would be hill sheep – so I was on Kirkstone Pass to meet him . . . when he was coming from Scotland. There was a thick white mist and the galloways were 2 miles off in it. He sent another gentleman afterwards. They said nothing about subsidy – I concluded they wanted to see what sort of cattle can be produced amongst the fells. Mr Hudson said some uncomplimentary things about the wasted grassland on the Borders; and I said a lot about the uselessness of trying to grow potatoes on a sheep farm – But potatoes he insists on having, he only laughed.

No doubt the minister was quite pleased to continue on his way after this confrontation – Beatrix could be a formidable opponent even though she was not well at the time. She really enjoyed her correspondence with local people on farming matters, especially Joe Moscrop and Mr Forrester, and it took her mind off her failing health.

George Forrester also remembered his father going to the dispersal sale of cattle at Troutbeck Park after Beatrix died. His father bought fifteen of the Galloways, and George went with him to collect them from Patterdale, where they had been 'walked' over the fell due to the difficulty of getting a large cattle truck to the farm. His father sold all but two of the cattle soon afterwards. The better of the two that he kept he named 'Beatrix' and exhibited it at six or seven local shows in 1947. She was Champion Galloway in every one of them – what a wonderful memorial to Beatrix Heelis!

Dennis Benson, mentioned in Chapter Seven and son of 'Tant' Benson, who was at Troutbeck Park for some years, remembered that sheep were also 'walked' to Hartsop Hall, between Kirkstone Pass and Ullswater, where they were sent for sale. He also remembered Tommy Christopherson bringing Beatrix's farm lorry to the farm to collect the wool after the clipping. It was a special treat for the children to accompany the lorry to Pickles, the wool merchants, in Kendal.

In the Lake District Beatrix Heelis was much better known as a Herdwick sheep breeder than as a writer of children's books. She really enjoyed chatting with the fell farmers, especially at the shepherds' meets and the agricultural shows, to which Willie usually uncomplainingly drove her. 'There is [she wrote], something very lovable about the silly sheep and the simple old-fashioned talk of those who work the soil and the flock.'

A local character who was a skilled drainer of wet areas remembered how, when he walked her land with her to see what needed to be done, she kept up with him even though he was much taller and stronger than she was. He offered to carry her over a rain-swollen beck, but she quickly took off her clogs and paddled through. The cold mountain water did not seem to worry her. She just dried her feet in a clump of long grass and continued on her way.

She was at her best with the local shepherds and country craftsmen. She often spoke to them in their own dialect, once turning on a farmer who wanted to talk to her about John Peel when she was busy judging some sheep, 'I never thought owt of John Peel myself.' She had little time for the county set. Above all she was kind and considerate to those who worked well. Two men, who had done a good job of repairing the roof at Castle Cottage, went over to the Tower Bank Arms nearby for a few drinks before returning home. Later when they came to be paid Beatrix congratulated them on a job well done, but told them she was worried they had ridden home to Troutbeck on their motor cycles after drinking. She said that they should have asked Walter Stevens to drive them home in her car.

Beatrix Heelis left 4,050 acres of farm land to the National Trust in her will, including Tilberthwaite Ghyll, Seathwaite Farm (614 acres), Penny Hill Farm, Eskdale (156 acres), Sawrey and Hawkshead (575 acres), land and houses at Coniston and Skelwith, farms and cottages at Medlock Vale, Daisy Nook (1,941 acres). It was one of the largest bequests ever made to the National Trust in the Lake District. When Willie died he bequeathed to the National Trust all the farms left to him on trust for his lifetime, and 258 acres of farmland at Tock How and High Wray near Hawkshead.

Susan Denyer, the Historic Buildings representative for the National Trust in the North West Region, sums up these bequests by saying that Beatrix Heelis was the right person at the right time. She had the foresight and the money, and she perceived the threats to the landscape and realised that through ownership and control the proper pattern of Lake District farming life could be safeguarded. Beatrix herself often disagreed with aspects of the Trust's work and did not always see eye-to-eye with their appointed agents, but she took a long-term view, saying, 'There are some silly mortals connected with it; but they will pass.'

It was typical of Beatrix that her handwritten notes for her will included instructions that the many items of oak furniture she had bought at local sales were to be left in the cottages and farmhouses she had given to the National Trust. She also added: 'No old horse or worn out dog to be sold; either given to a really trustworthy person or put down.'

CHAPTER NINE

LOOKING AFTER AN INVALID – ARTHUR JOHN HEELIS, RECTOR OF BROUGHAM

Another worry for Beatrix in the 1920s was that she had taken in to Castle Cottage Willie's brother, the Revd Arthur John, who had become too ill to continue the incumbency of Brougham near Penrith, or to live on alone in the rectory any longer. He was eccentric and at times difficult, but Beatrix had a soft spot for him since she and Willie had stayed at Brougham Rectory to support him at one of his annual Harvest Thanksgiving services. Like his grandfather before him at Long Marton, 'A.J.' farmed his own glebe. He never married, and was the owner of one of the first motor cars in the Eden Valley; the car often had to be pushed up hills.

He also bought one of the earliest cigarette lighters. His brothers made fun of this fancy newfangled gadget, but Arthur was very proud of it, so when out for a walk one day he

Arthur John Heelis, Rector of Brougham.

discovered that it had run dry he did not feel like returning home and admitting that it was not working – but he did want a smoke. Then suddenly he spotted an unattended motor bike. He had just removed the cap to the petrol tank and was dipping his lighter in when he heard the owner returning. In his hurry to replace the cap, he dropped the lighter into the petrol tank. He felt unequal to explaining the situation and ran away. It must have been a very bewildered biker who later investigated the mysterious knocking in his petrol tank!

His nieces, Isabel, Esther and Nancy Nicholson went over to the rectory occasionally to help clean the house or cook. Uncle Arthur, a bachelor, was rather slack about doing his washing up and went through his two or three tea and dinner sets until he no longer had any clean cups or plates left. His nieces were then called in to help out. Like his brothers he was a keen shooting man, and the nieces had to be extremely

Tom, Jane, Ada Isabella and Dr Jago (Jane's husband).

careful when cleaning and dusting as he was liable to leave loaded shotguns leaning up behind doors. One of his parishioners recalled his dangerous habit of walking through his fields using a loaded shotgun as a walking stick. Isabel was shocked one day to find a brace of dead hares hanging in a wardrobe in the bedroom.

The Harvest Thanksgiving that Willie and Beatrix were present at was also attended by a number of other Heelis relations, who came to dinner the night before attending the service the next day. They certainly included the George Heelises from Appleby, with their daughter, and James and Grace Nicholson from Kirkby Thore, and their daughters who used to clean up for 'A.J.'. Arthur had announced that dinner that night was to be rather special, a haunch of venison, and he told his guests that he had found a good cook in a girl he had met recently working in one of his potato fields. The various members of the family duly arrived, including Willie and Beatrix from Sawrey in their new car, which they were not too happy about driving across the rough track to the rectory. In due course everyone sat down to await the serving of dinner. Time went by, and as nothing seemed to be happening one of the ladies went out to the kitchen to see if any assistance was required. She found the dinner only half cooked and the cook lying helplessly drunk on the floor. The ladies had to rally round and finish the cooking themselves.

In a letter to Esther Nicholson in 1918, Beatrix wonders how Arthur, in those days of rationing, had managed to obtain a joint of meat, which Esther had told her she was going to cook for him. She asks: 'Has the Revd been killing a sheep on the sly?'

I have also seen an unpublished letter of Beatrix's mentioning this visit to Brougham and the fact that she was wearing a pair of high boots that were so tight she had to sit at the bottom of the stairs while her nieces Rosemary and Nancy attempted to pull them off. The letter is illustrated with little matchstick figures showing Rosemary as tall and thin and Nancy as short and squat struggling to remove the boots and finally pulling their aunt on to the floor! The whole story is told in the style of medieval knights of old, and it ends up with a carpenter being brought in to help!

I have the original of a letter to Grace Nicholson, which is included in the *Beatrix Potter's Letters* book. It is full of little humourous digs at people. The book dealer called Sharpe for instance, whom she says is 'appropriately named', and the remark, 'He [Arthur] admitted using one [a chair] which is

An extract from a letter by Beatrix to Grace Nicholson.

desired by Jane'. This is followed by the comment: 'Whether it is the only comfortable chair in the house, or whether he picked it because of Jane – I cannot say!' Arthur's sister Jane was in the habit of getting her own way, and Beatrix did not always agree with her.

The extract from this same letter that is of the greatest possible interest to me is the one where Beatrix, while discussing what should happen to various items of Arthur's in the rectory at Brougham at the time of his move to Sawrey, says: 'It seems that funny little man in the cocked hat is your grt grt grandfather. A J said Alick was going to take it in, I should think he will when he understands.'

The fact is that Alick (in fact my grandfather Alec) did take it in, and he, and later his widow and daughter Sylvie, had it at their house in Appleby for many years before it was handed down to me. It is now one of my proudest possessions, looking down from halfway up the stairs at my house in Milburn. It is well carved out of solid sandstone and is thought to have been done by a stonemason in Ravenstonedale. The likeness between the statue on page 72 and the picture on page 9 is striking.

It seems that Arthur's sale at Brougham raised about £600. Beatrix felt that some things were 'thrown away' and some were sold that he had wished to keep, but she had found it difficult to take in his wishes clearly and said she often made mistakes at sales, an admission with which many competing against her would be unlikely to agree! She bought a few things herself, including some chairs now at Hill Top. A set of seven chairs that Arthur had paid little more than £5 for made £54, which pleased him.

Beatrix got her nieces, Sylvie Heelis and Isabel Boazman, to pack up the books at Brougham Rectory after the sale. In a letter to Sylvie dated 22 July 1922, Beatrix says:

The man said he could put them loose in the car, but they get dreadfully battered by slipping out while being packed; they always will carry too many at once. I will post you a ball of binder twine – I should like to have had the presence of mind to buy more! The things were so good, and I was not overspent . . . I wish my coal box had included the pincers, I looked for them all through the sale . . . Mind they put plenty of rug round the uprights of the looking glass . . .

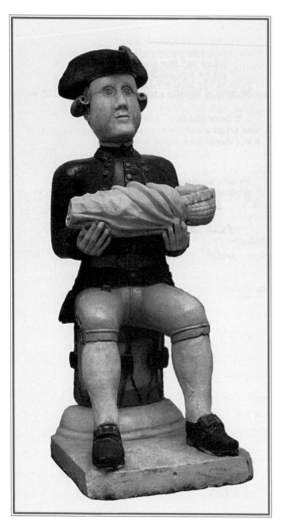

Statue of Thomas Heelis.

Beatrix was pleased with their efforts, writing to Sylvie a week later: 'Mr Brown arrived quite smiling about 7.30 and unloaded safely! . . . I think he [Uncle Arthur] is better in this sense – he dwells less continually on the past and on the future. My philosophy is to make the best of the present.'

Arthur's troubles seem to have been digestive and kidney, caused by a displacement from a bad operation for appendicitis some years earlier. When he moved into the bedroom above the kitchen at Castle Cottage it created problems when he had his bouts of illness as there was no inside sanitation. Beatrix also felt that he was a bit of a fire risk, and once caught him smoking a pipe under the bedclothes!

When he was well enough he used to enjoy going over the road to have a chat and a game of cards with Possy Postlethwaite. However, he got a chill in the summer of 1922 and had to stay in bed for a week. The nurse pronounced him very ill the first night and the doctor had to be consulted. Beatrix told Miss Choyce: 'He had a fancy to go to Silloth later on, where he is known at the hotel and looked after; then he will have to go back to his sisters at Appleby for a bit; but I fancy he will be glad to come back here in the spring. I don't want to keep him over the winter.'

He was still at Sawrey in December, and Beatrix wrote to Miss Choyce:

I am contending with the Revd, a curious situation – he is reinforced by my own good nature. I admit that it seems a shame to root him out, especially in bad weather! While it was fine we let him drift on, as it seemed better for him to be in the country. But it is *not* reasonable to keep him the year round. He had a wish to go to Blackpool, but the hydro is full over Xmas, when I particularly want to be free; I think Wm will run him over to his sisters at Appleby on the Saturday before Xmas, and afterwards he will go to Blackpool and then come back here. He is *very* much better; he always will be eccentric, and rather helpless. I don't dislike the prospect of his spending a good deal of his remaining days here (which he obstinately places at 2 yrs 6 weeks!!) but it is rather awkward in winter . . . His 'mind' has so far recovered as to admit holding political set to's with 'Possy' in the smithy and usually getting the best of it. He was very unwilling to go back Appleby direction; possibly rather shy after making such muddles of his affairs, which was not altogether excusable by bad health. His two elderly sisters [Blanche and May] came over one day last summer from Appleby and he bolted to Hawkshead, and stopped out till 8 o'clock! His preference for our society is touching; but excessive!

In the spring of 1923 Arthur John:

. . . crept about the village, looking very thin, but with a promising appetite. Then he got an influenza cold . . . I managed for a fortnight with Nurse Filkin's help, then he got worse last Sunday, and we got a nurse from Ulverston . . . His heart is weak and he might go suddenly; but myself I think he will last some time, wearing out by repeated illnesses. He is too ill to move at present, and it could only be to a nursing home if he went. It is rather a puzzle.

By the summer he was a little better: 'He won't dress or admit any improvement, but we occasionally hear his walking stick, clump clump along the passage upstairs, so he *can* walk.' He went to the Windermere nursing home when he was well enough to be moved, and returned to Castle Cottage in the spring of 1924. He had gained 7 lbs in weight, dressed well, and was 'quite a reformed character'. However, he soon got into bad habits again, 'sits in the dining room, with a rug, smoking a dirty clay pipe.' In a letter to Nancy in June 1925 Beatrix gave rather a good description of Arthur John in his latter days:

Uncle A.J. was brought home late, thanks to a bowling match; he lumbered in at the dining room window with his torn old scarf, a dusty waterproof and his hat on the back of his fuzzy hair – demanding library books and a hot water bottle. Miss Choyce who hadn't seen him since his beard grew exploded in amusement. A.J. was very angry – went to bed – and was sick! He is nearly as usual now after fasting – but he still says that a channel between his liver and his stomach is blocked in such a manner that the juices etc. I should say it is too many cakes and puddings, and a little jealousy of Uncle Alick [Alec Heelis, his eldest brother]; he doesn't like to hear of anyone else having operations and himself left out of it.

In warm weather he had in the past often gone out shooting rabbits, and he used to visit the reading room at Hawkshead, but the cold and damp finally got him down. He had further spells in bed, attended by the district nurse and Dr Brownlie from Windermere. He was uncomplaining and patient, and sat indoors a lot reading or playing chess by himself. He died in January 1926: 'Our poor invalid Arthur Heelis has peacefully fallen asleep. It is a release for him, and will be a relief when one gets used to it.'

CHAPTER TEN

Visits to Sawrey by the Nicholson Nieces

Previous mention of Esther and Nancy Nicholson, their brothers and their mother Grace (née Heelis) leads me on to the special relationship between Nancy and her aunt. She was in fact Willie's goddaughter, but of course Beatrix adopted her as her own. Beatrix also took a great interest in Willie's godson, Colin, his brother George's son, who went to prep school at The Craig at Windermere, and spent much of his spare time from school coming over on the ferry to be with Willie and Beatrix in Sawrey.

But Nancy's relationship was much more special, though it started off unfortunately. Shortly after their marriage in 1913, Willie and Beatrix drove over to Kirkby Thore to take tea with the Nicholsons at Ashton Lea, the house that James Nicholson had inherited from his mother. Grace sat at the head of a long refectory table with the silver kettle and teapot in front of her and Beatrix and Willie on either side of her. James Nicholson sat at the other end of the table with Nancy, the youngest by ten years of the Nicholson children, on his right and Richard (Dick) on his left. Dick was dressed ready to go off and play football. On either side of the middle of the table were seated Isabel and Christopher. Esther was away at the time. To amuse his little sister, Dick took a cap out of his pocket on which he had painted a face. He placed this over his knee, which he raised above the side of the table. Nancy, who had her mouth full at the time, exploded with laughter which did not amuse her father. He lashed out at Dick, whose nose began to bleed (a Nicholson weakness). Beatrix remained impassive but Willie was visibly upset and the tea party broke up in chaos.

Undeterred by this incident, Willie and Beatrix later invited Grace and Nancy to stay at Sawrey after they had settled in at Castle Cottage. It had not been ready when they returned from their honeymoon and they had been living in temporary accommodation in the village, but now the extra rooms were complete and all was ready. Nancy was about six at the time, a

A Heelis and Nicholson family group. Back row, left to right: Alec, Aday, Guy Hopes, George, Grace Nicholson, Willie. Middle row: Blanche, Sybil holding Rosemary, Hylton, Christopher, Isabel and Esther Nicholson. Front row: Sylvie, -?-, -?-.

rather shy little girl. Imagine her embarrassment when her mother found that she had got the date for the visit wrong. The result was that after an exhausting walk from Windermere ferry, they discovered on arrival at Castle Cottage that the spare room was already occupied by George's wife, Sybil, and her daughter Rosemary, and that the Nicholsons were not in fact expected till the next day. They were, of course, otherwise accommodated for the first night and had a very pleasant stay, Nancy seeming to hit it off with her aunt right from the start. They told each other stories, Beatrix concentrating on Nancy rather than the grown-ups, whose conversation bored her. They planted water lilies at Moss Eccles tarn above Sawrey on one of their walks.

Nancy was not very much older when her mother asked her one day if she would like to stay with her aunt and uncle again, this time on her own. Grace was surprised when she accepted immediately, because she was normally so shy that she clung to her mother's skirt or hid under a bed when strangers were about. She spent several hours under a bed once on a visit to Aunt Jane in London, who was looking after her while her mother went shopping. Jane could not persuade her to come out, nor could she get under the bed to pull her out. She did not think to use the method her father used at home, which was to hook her out with a walking stick.

On this second visit to Sawrey Nancy was delivered to Castle Cottage and, shortly afterwards, Beatrix and Willie drove her mother back to Kirkby Thore. After the car had gone Nancy had a whale of a time with Mrs Rogerson, the housekeeper, and a girl she knew as Miney. At home Nancy was sent off to bed on her own, but now she had two grown-ups to show off to, and show off she did. After a hot bath she danced around with very little on except a necklace, and delayed going to bed. Beatrix was not pleased with her at breakfast the next morning and announced that Uncle Willie would have to 'deal with her'. His punishment was to give her sums to do, little realising that Nancy really enjoyed sums, so it was no great punishment, only a nuisance to her poor uncle who had to set them!

Over numerous visits Nancy, sometimes accompanied by Esther, felt that Beatrix handled her very well and brought out the best in her. She never fussed her, told her stories, and thought up simple and interesting things for her to do. Beatrix and Nancy tended to gang up on Willie, who rather lent himself to being teased, but he did not really seem to mind. Beatrix wrote letters to Nancy and to her mother frequently, and took a great interest in Nancy's schooling. She also wrote to her sister Esther, and had the occasional visit from the eldest Nicholson girl, Isabel. Nancy confirmed that it was herself and her sisters who acted as guinea pigs in trying out the early designs of Beatrix's board games. An example of a picture letter written by Beatrix to Nancy describes Willie and Beatrix being turned out of a first class railway carriage at Kirkby Stephen station near Appleby.

In the summer of 1922 Beatrix and Willie's visitors included Willie's brother George and his son and daughter, Colin and Rosemary. A

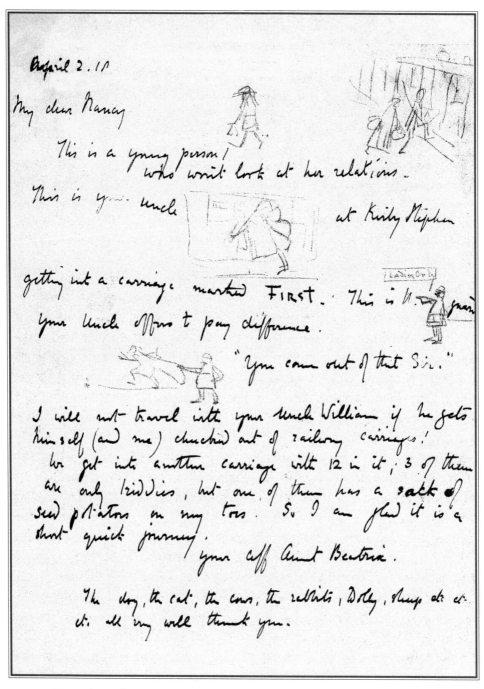

April 2.10

My dear Nancy

This is a young person!
who won't look at her relations.

This is your uncle
at Kirby Stephen

getting into a carriage marked FIRST. This is
your Uncle offers to pay difference.

"You come out of that Sir."

I will not travel with your Uncle William if he gets
himself (and me) chucked out of railway carriages!
he got into another carriage with 12 in it; 3 of them
are only kiddies, but one of them has a sack of
seed potatoes on my toes. So I am glad it is a
short quick journey.
your aff Aunt Beatrix.

The dog, the cat, the cows, the rabbits, Dolly, sheep et et
et. all very well thank you.

Picture letter from Beatrix to Nancy Nicholson, the 'young person' illustrated.

little later Esther and Nancy came accompanied by their eldest brother, Richard:

> . . . a fine fellow and a terrible fisherman, he is going to British Columbia, seems to have an opening and knows a little already of fruit growing. He had some outlandish Canadian lake flies; and he and Uncle Willie by moonlight caught – or poached – trout in such numbers up at the tarn that I rebelled. They were red, likely salmon, and made me think of the revolt of the London apprentices in the middle ages against a salmon diet. We daren't give them away and it was no weather for posting fish, so they put back quantities. The biggest weighed lbs 3 . . . I never saw such ugly black monsters. I think they must feed on tadpoles in the mud. The village people don't know there are fish in the tarn, and it is not advisable to enlighten them. The young people were very merry and their visits were a success in spite of the weather.

Nancy remembered how she and Esther used to row the boat to the little island with a single rowan tree on it, and that Esther painted the name *Mary Rose* on the boat, inspired by the J.M. Barrie play of that name, popular at the time. She was also warned about jumping from tuft to tuft of the heather by the tarn, as her aunt told her there were adders there.

Nancy remembered an amusing incident when she was helping Beatrix in the cornfields at Sawrey when old Mrs Potter, Beatrix's mother, drove up one day in a smart open landau, looking rather like Queen Victoria, with her coachman in front and a young boy behind. When Rupert Potter was still alive the coachman used to wear white breeches and top boots, and the coats had brass buttons with the Potter crest on them. Even now the coachman and the boy were very smartly dressed in all black livery. Beatrix was cross as she wanted to get on with the harvesting, but her mother insisted on talking to her, so Beatrix grabbed two sheaves of corn and got into the carriage beside her with the sheaves under her arms, to the consternation of her mother and the coachman.

Mrs Potter lived in some style at Lindeth Howe. In fact, she was the last person in the South Lakes area to have a landau drawn by a pair of horses. She visited Beatrix weekly and usually stayed precisely one hour. It caused some amusement in Hawkshead when the story got round that Beatrix called on her mother one day in her working clothes. A new maid, not recognising her, refused her entry and said that Mrs Potter was not receiving visitors that afternoon. Beatrix is said to have swept past remarking, 'I think she will when she sees who it is!'

One summer day Beatrix took Esther and Nancy through the Grizedale Forest to pick up a pig for Hill Top Farm. The pig was probably bought from Sally Scales, who lived at Stott Farm in the woods, about a mile from Graythwaite, from where many of the Hill Top pigs were bought. It was Sally Scales on whom Beatrix based Sally Benson, the old woman in her book *Wag-by-Wall*. Beatrix drove them in a 'tub cart' pulled by her favourite pony, Dolly. She always liked to drive herself on these occasions. On the return journey the pig was in the back with Esther sitting over it with her legs on the sides, while Nancy rode up front with her aunt. It conjures up rather a nice picture of the sort of relationship Beatrix had with these young people. Of course Esther and Nancy enjoyed their stays at Sawrey as they had a much freer life than they had at home in Kirkby Thore. They could run round the farm to their hearts' content, or row the boat on Moss Eccles tarn, Willie's favourite fishing place. Nancy also remembers how much she enjoyed playing the pianola at Castle Cottage very loudly on Sundays, when the villagers were going to church.

In 1916 Beatrix had written a story specially for Nancy called *The Oakmen*, based on stories they told each other while walking through the fields and woods. Many of Beatrix's letters to Nancy continued *The Oakmen* story. One such reads:

> I have been cross cutting firewood from a large broken oaktree . . . A little robin has been watching us all day, hopping on the logs. He was so tame he nearly touched us – He had very bright little beady eyes, and a very red cap – no, not a cap, a red waistcoat. I did not feel quite sure whether he was a real robin, till he found a worm in some rotten bark . . . He kept flying round behind the tree, to speak to some one, and coming back. He came back dozens of times and I had nothing for him – except a bit of apple. He went home before we did on accnt of chilblains on his toes. I believe he lives with the Oakmen. At all events he had supper with them. He sat on a chair with his feet in hot water and ate pickled caterpillars out of a pie dish!

Many years later she asked to borrow *The Oakmen* story back for possible use in something she was working on. In fact she did not use it, and mislaid it. After Beatrix died Nancy thought never to see it again. Still later Nancy heard that Leslie Linder had acquired a lot of Beatrix's writings and drawings from Commander Kenneth Duke and his wife Stephanie, Beatrix's cousin, who had inherited them. She wrote to find out if Leslie Linder had found *The Oakmen* among the papers he had acquired. He had indeed found it and, with typical understanding and generosity, returned it to her. It turned out that Beatrix no longer felt able to do the detailed illustrations herself, and so negotiated with a Mr Ernest Aris to do some. Beatrix and Mr Aris didn't hit it off – in one of her letters she calls him a 'bounder' – but the main reason she did not send it in for publication was that she feared that the story was partly based on something that Nancy

One of Ernest Aris's illustrations for *The Oakmen*.
Courtesy of the V & A Museum.

had read elsewhere, and she could not risk a possible breach of copyright. Mr Aris's drawings and the correspondence between him and Beatrix are in the Beatrix Potter collection at the Victoria and Albert Museum. Nancy recently presented her original copy of *The Oakmen* to the same museum.

In 1917 there was some communication between Beatrix's publishers and Mr Aris's publishers regarding a character called 'Peter Rabbit' in a book Mr Aris had written called *The Treasure Seekers*. Warnes claimed infringement of copyright. Mr Aris stated in a letter to Beatrix that he had never heard of her book *Peter Rabbit*! He even asked her to give him a copy of her book as he felt it would be interesting to compare 'the two Peters'. It is hardly surprising that relations between them were somewhat cool!

Beatrix told Nancy most of the stories in *The Fairy Caravan* while she was writing it, and they often looked at the animals described there together. Beatrix was amused by a comment of Nancy's when she was quite small and they were looking at some cows. Beatrix explained the finer points required in a good animal. After a pause Nancy commented, 'I likes a "coo" with a big bag!' As Nancy got older and began reading more grown-up stories she found it more difficult to take as much interest or to make as useful comments to Beatrix as she would have liked on the stories Beatrix tried out on her.

Nancy only remembered one occasion when her aunt was cross with Esther and herself. It upset Nancy, but she felt it was deserved. Esther, ten years older than Nancy, had suggested it might be a good idea to do some weeding in the orchard while their aunt was out, and they set to with more enthusiasm than skill. Unfortunately most of the 'weeds' they pulled up had been specially planted by Beatrix as a collection of wild flowers from the surrounding countryside.

Beatrix was angry with Nancy's brother Dick for causing a pony he had ridden all the way over from Kirkby Thore in the Eden Valley to Sawrey to get a nasty sore on its back. Normally, however, Beatrix got on well with Dick. On one occasion she sent him and Nancy and Esther off for the afternoon to Esthwaite with a picnic tea. They 'trawled' for fish all round the outside edge of the lake several times. Plenty of perch were caught – most having to be put back as too small. No one believed Nancy when she said she had got a bite, but she was right and they were soon helping her in a fight with a decent-sized pike. They had no landing net, so the contents of the picnic basket were emptied and the pike was successfully landed using the basket. Nancy, the baby of the party, went up in their estimation.

The three of them also went off another day with Miss Choyce to Little Langdale. Miss Choyce was supposed to be in charge of Nancy, the youngest, and bring her back before the others, but Nancy ran ahead and Miss Choyce had to return without her.

During the same week the three Nicholsons were sitting down to a meal at Castle Cottage with Willie, Beatrix and Arthur. Arthur suddenly got up and went into the next room before returning to the table. While he was out Beatrix turned to Nancy and whispered to her, 'He's gone to get his teeth!' During another mealtime an argument developed between Willie and Arthur about fishing techniques. Arthur went out and came back with a full-sized fishing rod to try and prove his point. The rod was so long that he had to be partly outside the dining room door. The children and Beatrix found this most amusing and exchanged looks.

Another of Nancy's memories of Sawrey was of regular calls on Mr and Mrs Mackereth when he was still the shepherd at Hill Top. Nancy and her sister would sit beside Mr Mackereth while he had his 'elevenses'. She recalled their cottage as being close to Hill Top, with another of Beatrix's cottages closer to it. Beatrix considered the tenant of the latter cottage very left wing (in fact decidedly 'red'). Beatrix allotted him a special apple tree with very red apples on it from which he could help himself, but on no account was he to touch the other trees!

Beatrix never drove a car herself. She was always driven by Willie in his own little car, or chauffeur-driven in her car. Nancy recalls Willie being a very slow and careful driver, rarely travelling at any sort of speed. He sometimes used to stall on hills and Esther and Nancy had to jump out, take a stone from the wall, and put it under one of the rear wheels. Once while travelling up a particularly steep hill, smoke started coming up through the floorboards and Willie shouted to his nieces to be prepared to bale out in a hurry if it burst into flames. Willie's car was a Wolseley 'Hornet', which he changed for a new one in 1931 in a complicated swap. The old car went to Nurse Edwards, whose unreliable old Morris went in part exchange. Beatrix was at a loss as to how to explain this at the AGM of her local Nursing Association.

Ann Fearnhill recalls that one of the less conventional sports in which her Uncle Willie very occasionally indulged was catching pheasants with his car! When he saw a pheasant sitting on the road he would coast up very quietly to within a few yards, then accelerate suddenly and blast his horn. He timed this so perfectly that the unfortunate bird broke its neck on the windscreen and didn't get squashed.

Beatrix continued to take a great interest in Willie's godson, Colin Heelis, long after he left The Craig School at Windermere. When he was working with the Argentine Railways between the wars he became a fluent Spanish speaker and Beatrix sent him copies of her books as they were translated into Spanish. When war was declared he returned to England and joined the RAF. When he went back to Argentina after the war the railways were nationalised and he lost his job. This was bad enough, but he also found that his luggage had been tampered with and all his signed copies of Beatrix's little books had disappeared.

CHAPTER ELEVEN

GETTING OLDER – MR AND MRS HEELIS OF SAWREY

Beatrix and Willie were a very devoted couple, and they got on well together. She found him untidy about the house, he always seemed to be getting holes in his socks, he snored at night and he got deafer as he got older but she knew she could not change him. Willie found her domineering but did not usually seem to mind and never complained. He half killed himself, especially during the war years when he had very little help in the office, in keeping all her farm accounts and income tax claims in his own hand. They annoyed each other at times and Beatrix was able to let herself go in her marvellous letters to friends. When she does criticise Willie in a letter it is usually rather tongue-in-cheek, as when she wrote to Nancy Nicholson in 1918, 'He is a very heartless man. I was stung by a wasp – (where I sit down). It was in my bath towel; and when I called to your Uncle William who was safe in bed asleep – he calmly said "It doesn't matter" and went on sleeping.' In a letter to Nancy's mother, Grace, she said 'I flatter myself that I have learnt to make hay, without advice from a party who plays golf till 7 pm on a workable Saturday. It is a little annoying to be lectured when one has been breaking one's back . . .'.

Willie had no such outlet and bottled things up, but he could always go off shooting or fishing, or to play bowls or golf, or take part in country dancing. Overall they were well suited. He shared her passion for Sawrey, the surrounding area and the simple life. She understood and appreciated his country tastes, his gentle manner and leisurely attitude and his pleasure in his favourite sports. Above all she appreciated the courteous manner in which he conducted her affairs and his business.

It was nice that Willie and Beatrix were often able to relax together. In a letter to Miss Choyce dated 17 June 1924 Beatrix wrote:

> Friday, Saturday were glorious hot days, Sunday cold and drizzle, now today, Tuesday, is a hot windy day again . . .

Prize-winning bowler, Willie, at Hawkshead.

Yesterday evening was the first really warm night. Mr Heelis and I fished (at least I rowed!) till darkness; coming down the lane about 11. It was lovely on the tarn, not a breath of wind and no midges. The fish were 'taking short', running at the fly without getting hooked, but he caught 4 which was plenty. We put back the smallest, the other 3 weighed over 4 lbs together, the biggest was 1 lb 10 ozs. They were exciting to catch as they fought and made rushes to get under the boat.

In April 1937 Willie was able to get away for a short period during which time he visited a tailor. Beatrix wrote to Nancy, 'Uncle Willie continues much better for his visit to Liverpool, and his gorgeous clothes have arrived, and fit round the neck. I am not sure whether the blue check on gray [sic] may be a little light coloured. The overcoat is very handsome and suitable for a large important figure. Nurse made him put on the coat for her inspection. The shirts are very nice. I refuse to believe that the underwear is "all wool".' The next year Beatrix went on a holiday to the same nurse, by then retired. She wrote to Nancy, 'Your Uncle must have written in woebegone style! I abandoned him for eleven days for the first time in more than 25 years!! The spinsters next door reported that he had taken it to heart. I went to stay with Nurse Edwards at High Bebington, Wirral, than which I never saw a more uninteresting spot, but it was good air, and I lay in bed and got rid of my sciatica . . . I feel quite myself again, but the weather is so bad – so now I shall have to be careful of getting damp this winter. Nurse has a tolerable little house, convenient, especially the gas cooker – buses past the door and aeroplanes over the back garden. I am a country mouse, like Timmy Willy.'

Josephine Banner gave a wonderful picture of a visit by Beatrix to the farm in Little Langdale where she and her husband, the artist Delmar Banner, were living at that time. Beatrix's old car could not get up the steep farm road, so the farmer provided a milk float with a grey pony. She walked up a board into the float holding the Banners' hands on either side, took the reins and rode up in a triumphal procession with the cottagers waving to her as she went by. On arrival at the farm, Josephine told me that Beatrix insisted on visiting all the farm animals and outbuildings. She then sat down to a very good lunch, having second helpings of everything. Josephine kept saying to me, 'She was so pretty,' and, 'She was the youngest and bonniest old lady I have ever met.'

Beatrix really enjoyed attending local furniture auction sales but I have no record of Willie ever attending one with her. She bought many old pieces of oak furniture such as court cupboards and dressers for both Hill Top and the farmhouses she had acquired. It was said that if she was determined to buy a piece 'she held her arm resolutely aloft, and it was not lowered until every other bidder fell out'. Willie accompanied her to farm sales, always being ready to advise her on any technical points. There were complications sometimes when Willie's firm acted both for Beatrix and the other party.

In one of her letters to Miss Choyce she starts off:

Have I-a-fool-of-myself-at-a-sale made? I do not know, I cannot tell! The advt in the Gazette announced several cows, an aged black mare . . . a calf, hay mows etc etc and 'a portion of household furniture'. It was a little out of the way farm near Crook, a forlorn dirty little place, everyone dead except an old man removed to the infirmary. My purpose was to buy the calf, a nice little red heifer, which we obtained for £3 and stowed into the back seat of the car.

I poked into a dark little kitchen and amongst broken chairs & lumber beheld a carved and dated dark oak court cupboard. I suppose it had been too lumbersome to remove with the other 'portion of household furniture'. I had vain hopes that I was going to get a bargain – no dealers. But there is no such thing as bargains in this district; there appeared two other knowledgeable people – a second auctioneer, R D Dickinson, and an unknown lady & gentleman; between them I paid £21-10 . . . Unquestionably it is genuine and untouched – except by rats. It did not seem to be wormy . . . The doors fastened with little wooden buttons. The carving was rather rough . . . It had belonged to the aged wife, the neighbours said she had refused good offers in her lifetime for the 'sideboard'.

A pencilled note written after Beatrix had got it home reads: 'I think it is a very good cupboard, horribly dirty, but it will polish alright, except for some clumpy later hinges and a drop corner damaged . . . it is in good condition. I must keep away from sales for some time!'

Generous in so many ways, she was nevertheless keen on a bargain and kept strict control over the household budget. She would want her 'luck money' at sheep auctions, and was known to have demanded a rebate after buying some sheep dip, as she said her prize-winning Herdwicks were a good advertisement to her suppliers! Mrs Rogerson confirmed what Tom Storey had said about Castle Cottage being the last house in the village to have electric light. 'Mrs Heelis would use a candle while she was writing before her husband came in for tea. Then the oil lamps were turned on. I wasn't surprised that her eyes began to fail. She used to say that maids who weren't prepared to trim the lamps and keep them clean and wanted electric light instead could leave!' Beatrix wouldn't even allow Mrs Rogerson to have a wireless set. If she felt that too much was being spent on the housekeeping she would tell Mrs Rogerson that 'she'd end up in the workhouse'.

Beatrix was related to the Gaddums of Burneside near Kendal. Mrs Rogerson recalled in her old age the occasion when Beatrix attended the Gaddums' golden wedding dinner party. Beatrix put on a smart old dress for the occasion and also wore her best jewellery for the last time. When she got home she could not undo her buttons and Willie was not available so she spent the rest of the night in the dress until Mrs Rogerson rescued her on arriving for work the next morning. Beatrix's cousin, Stephanie Duke, inherited Beatrix's jewellery after she died, but a lot of it was later stolen in London.

Beatrix had often worried about what would happen to Willie if she were to die first. When she was in hospital in Liverpool in 1939 for a serious operation she worried so much that she wrote to Miss Hammond and Miss Mills, who lived next door to Castle Cottage, saying: 'If it was not for poor W H I would be indifferent to the result. It is such a wonderfully easy going under; and in some ways preferable to a long invalidism, with only old age to follow . . .'.

She then went on to mention various things she would want moved from Castle Cottage to Hill Top and what should happen to the Pekingese dogs: 'I hope that Cecily [Miss Mills] and Wm will walk out little dogs on Saturdays; they are old enough to face comment! *Could* she learn piquet, or could you play 3 handed whist? It would be better for the poor man to . . . re-marry . . . I hope and feel sure you will do your best for him in the winter evenings.'

Willie felt the strain of travelling back and forth visiting her in hospital, but did so uncomplainingly. Beatrix must have felt glad that she and Willie had decided to let Miss Hammond and Miss Mills have the cottage next door. They had done so because it was so much on top of them and they wanted someone there they knew and trusted, but now it would be useful in the event of one dying before the other. Beatrix did not in fact die till 22 December 1943, and mercifully it was at home and not in hospital. Willie was lost without her, but he knew her wishes. Neither of them was particularly religious. Beatrix, the daughter of Dissenter parents, rather leant towards the Quakers and was known to have attended the Meeting House at Colthouse near Hawkshead. She certainly had no truck with a local Church of England parson who had said that animals had no souls!

In May 1923 Beatrix recalled a visit from the local parson: 'Just had a call from Revd McNally to enquire after A J H [Arthur John], most polite & agreeable, & me with a conscience that I have not contributed to the augmentation of stipend fund. What ever is to be done! I will tell W H [Willie] that he must subscribe . . .'. But adds the rider: 'in moderation.'

Margaret Lane found Willie very difficult to get on with when interviewing him as a widower. She really only got his co-operation after virtually losing her temper with him. In fairness I believe he was by then a tired and lonely man, who remembered how

Willie at Castle Cottage with one of the Pekinese dogs.

much Beatrix had shunned publicity in her lifetime, and he just could not come to terms with answering so many personal questions. He and Beatrix had done so much for so many of their relations, especially the nephews and nieces, but sadly none of them were able to come forward to look after him as she and Willie had done with Arthur John. Beatrix had been the dominant partner, as she pointed out to her friends on more than one occasion, and she had the money. Now that he was on his own he was not going to be bullied by a writer, especially a lady, and he still felt in his heart of hearts that Beatrix would not approve of the publicity and adulation that was about to be let loose. He died before Margaret Lane's book was published, but would undoubtedly have approved of it.

The Quaker Meeting House, Colthouse near Hawkshead.

Margaret Lane wrote to Willie's brother George after Willie died:

Mr Heelis's death, as you may imagine, is a source of great personal regret to me. It is most sadly disappointing that now when my life of Beatrix Potter is finished, he is not alive to see it. I have looked forward to reading it to him this winter, as we planned; I believe it would have pleased and satisfied him; he had spared no trouble to put the fullest possible material in my hands, and as our association had been a most pleasant one, I believe that he, too, looked forward to the final stages . . .

Willie was a sick man at the end, and found trying to run both the office and the farms too much for him. Farm incomes were so low at that time that he even had to dispense with Joe Moscrop. Instead of the usual bargaining conducted by Beatrix, Willie told him the wage he asked, in addition to his board and lodging, was impossible. A sad note on which to end Joe's long connection with the Heelis family, though Willie told him he was very sorry.

Letter to Willie from the Herdwick Sheep-Breeders' Association on the death of Beatrix.

Whether or not Beatrix would have enjoyed the publicity that followed her death, and the interest in her life that has increased year by year all over the world since, must remain a mystery.

She certainly shunned publicity in her lifetime. She did not intend her *Journal* to be published, and had invented her own code to keep it private, but I do not think she would have minded the code being broken by Leslie Linder, as he turned out to be one of her most devoted admirers, and was responsible for ensuring that so much original material remained in this country – mostly now at the Victoria and Albert Museum. The *Journal* makes very good reading and gives an interesting insight into the period for which she kept it. She may well have wanted to follow on in the tradition of other well-known diarists of the past, whose works she had admired. She

An illustration of Herdwicks in *The Fairy Caravan*.
© Frederick Warne & Co., 1929, 1992.

may also have been not altogether averse to the *Journal* being published, as she left several clues to enable the code to be broken.

She must have guessed that she would be idolised after her death because she spent much of her final years in annotating her papers and sorting them out for possible biographers. I possess the rough draft in her own handwriting of part of her will, in which she sensed that Hill Top would become a sort of shrine to her memory and her work. She confirmed what she had already briefly mentioned to Miss Hammond and Miss Mills regarding her possessions to be moved from Castle Cottage. She went to great pains to specify which items of furniture, china, pictures, drawings and books should be included, and how they should be displayed.

> I would like certain favourite pieces of furniture to be kept for Hill Top (in the event of it seeming likely that my rooms there are preserved) namely the Chippendale glass-fronted bureau at present in the Library here [Castle Cottage] – (the first piece of antique furniture I bought); and the 3 Chippendale single chairs in the dining room here, and the pair of Shield back chairs . . . The little [chair] in my bedroom which belonged to great grandmother Alice Crompton also to Hill Top . . . My good china to go into the bureau and corner cupboard at Hill Top. The sampler opposite my bed to hang in the oak room at Hill Top between the four-poster and the fireplace. . . . The looking glass with ivory knobs which belonged to my great grandmother, Alice Hayhurst Crompton, together with the small chest of drawers which it stands on, I wish to be put in the north bedroom at Hill Top (over parlour) . . .

I think she might well have been amused by the fuss made since her death, but I doubt whether she would have approved of a lot of the theorising and psychoanalysing that has been published. She had told Graham Greene when he wrote an article on a 'dark period in Miss Potter's art', that she deprecated sharply 'the Freudian school' of criticism. Nor did she and Willie take kindly to a newspaper article in 1924 referring to Beatrice Webb (the social reformer – also née Potter), 'whom many of us remember as the writer of children's books when she was Miss Beatrix Potter'.

Beatrix decided that the time had come to act firmly and she wrote to Warnes:

> I enclose copy of a letter which I am posting to the Editor of the Sunday Herald . . . I usually take no notice, as even the insult of being mistaken for Mrs. Webb is preferable to publicity. But if the Webbs are going to become prominent along with our new rulers, the error had better be contradicted; for I do not think that nice old-fashioned people who like my books would like them quite so much if they believed them to be of socialist origin.

Willie was annoyed with the portrait of Mr and Mrs Webb on the front page of the *Sunday Herald*. In a letter to Miss Choyce, Beatrix says: 'The papers print the untruth prominently, and the contradiction so unprominently that it has no effect to stop the lie. The most laughable part of it was a photograph of Beatrix Potter and her husband – a horrid little fat man with a billy goat beard! Wm was furious, and said it was a libel on *him*.'

Beatrix goes on to suggest that the best form of contradiction might be to get photographed beside a favourite pig or cow and get it inserted in one of the 'genteel newspapers'! She, in fact, had a pig that often stood on its hind legs leaning over the pig sty: 'But it's hanging up, unphotographed and cured now.'

I wonder if it was the same pig that Willie rubbed cream of tartar into instead of saltpetre, thus discolouring the hams for that year. One is also reminded of another of Beatrix's letters: 'The portrait of two pigs arm in arm – looking at the sun-rise – is *not* a portrait of me and Mr Heelis, though it is a view of where we used to walk on Sunday afternoons! When I want to put William in a book – it will have to be as some very tall thin animal.'

Willie had every right to feel cross about Beatrix being referred to as Mrs Sidney Webb, especially when he was stopped in the street in Ambleside one day and asked if his wife had married again!

There is no doubt that in spite of many ups and downs, Beatrix remained absolutely loyal to her publishers, Warnes. She rewarded them by leaving the copyrights on her books to the Warne family. I have the letter written to Willie two days after Beatrix died from Arthur L. Stephens, the then managing director of the company:

Dear Mr Heelis

I was very sorry to learn that Mrs Heelis had passed away.

There are still working with me at the office four or five members of the staff who were there at the time when 'The Tale of Peter Rabbit' was first published. Actually, although I began business life at Bedford Street fifty five years ago, I was not working there when the first of those little books was produced, but I rejoined the association when the business became a Joint-Stock Company.

Being connected through my father's second marriage with the Warne family I know the history of the business from its beginning and it is largely owing to this that I am so well able to appreciate how loyally Mrs Heelis kept to her first publisher, through dark days, and since the time that it fell to me to take control of the business, I have greatly appreciated her continued pleasant association. I have always felt there was a debt due to her for her great loyalty and I have done my best to acknowledge it – I hope I have not altogether failed.

Those of us members of the business who remember the day when Mrs Heelis's stories first appeared, are all getting on in years and we know we must soon give up, but, as long as we are spared, we shall feel proud to know that we have been connected with her and it is with that thought which makes us sad that she has been called away.

With this feeling, we wish to express our sincere sympathy with you in your loss.

Yours sincerely.

Arthur L. Stephens

When Willie himself died at the age of seventy-three the *Westmorland Gazette* gave him the following tribute:

His more intimate friends breaking through a somewhat reserved disposition, found in him a real companion, a hidden reserve of humour, kindness and consideration, but at all times shunning ostentation. He faithfully maintained the quiet dignity becoming an English gentleman, which ably befitted him for the great respect and esteem in which he was held over a wide area in North Lancashire, Westmorland and Cumberland . . . He was interested in everything locally, and although reserved, he was a very shrewd man, with a kindly manner, and he would be remembered with affection.

A LITTLE CRY FROM THE BACK OF THE TOWN HALL AT HAWKSHEAD

Whether Beatrix intended it or not, Hill Top became more and more popular with the public down the years. So much so that the National Trust had to try and find another building to take some of the stress away from Hill Top, and where the drawings could be better preserved and shown in controlled conditions.

A highly suitable house seemed to be Belmount Hall at Hawkshead, bought by Beatrix after its eccentric owner, Miss Rebecca Owen, a Thomas Hardy fan and an admirer of Mussolini, had died in Italy. Various uses had been proposed for it in Beatrix's lifetime as she was not keen to leave it unoccupied for too

Belmount Hall, Hawkshead.

David Heelis, John Heelis and Jean Holland, daughter of Beatrix's cousin, Stephanie, at the Beatrix Potter Exhibition in the Tate Gallery, London.

long. She had hoped that it might be made into a rest home for aged evacuees by the Society of Friends, but they could not raise the money. Beatrix had the roof repaired, and was delighted with the daffodils and azaleas in the deserted garden. She finally left it to the National Trust, but when they tried to get planning permission for a gallery there many years later it was turned down because of the dangerous access from the main road. It is now a guest house.

Willie and Jack Heelis had left the Hawkshead solicitor's office to the Trust when their successors, Gatey and Heelis, felt they needed it no longer. In the 1980s the partners decided to concentrate on the Ambleside office, so allowing the Hawkshead office to go to the Trust. Careful plans were drawn up to create a gallery which would be suitable for showing off a certain number of the drawings each year, and aspects of Beatrix's farming and conservation interests, while retaining the atmosphere of the old solicitor's office. Susan Denyer, the local National Trust Historic Buildings adviser, kindly asked me down to see

Two of the author's grandchildren, Sarah and Rebecca.

how it was getting on. I took with me a number of old family photo albums and she selected several for display and for use in the visitors' brochure.

I have happy memories of 28 July 1988 when the new Beatrix Potter Gallery at Hawkshead was officially opened. I travelled down with my son, Guy, and his wife and their youngest daughter Emma, then just six weeks old. My other two granddaughters, Sarah and Rebecca, remained behind in Appleby. Colin Heelis's son, Michael, with his wife Judith, were also guests. As so often happens in the Lakes the rain lashed down all day, but it did not mar a very happy occasion for the large numbers attending. Halfway through the speeches in Hawkshead Town Hall, a little cry came up from the carrycot at the back of the hall, but Emma was soon comforted and quietened down by her father. It did not interfere with the formalities, and everyone seemed amused and delighted that the youngest Heelis present, Beatrix and Willie's great-great-great-niece, had thus asserted herself. After all Beatrix had said, 'I began to assert myself at 70.' Emma was starting a bit earlier!

The speeches ended and we set off under umbrellas to the old Heelis office. The Trust had had the inspired idea of getting Geoff Storey, Tom's son and successor at Hill Top, to declare the gallery open by cutting a strand of

Nancy Hudson (née Nicholson) with Emma Heelis, on Nancy's eightieth birthday.

Judith Heelis with her prize-winning Herdwick at the Great Yorkshire Show, 1993.

Herdwick wool stretched across the front doors with a pair of sheep shears. One felt that the President of the Herdwick Sheep-Breeders' Association was surely looking down with approval. I am sure too that Beatrix would be delighted to know that another generation of Heelises have become fond of Herdwick sheep. At the Great Yorkshire Show in 1993 at Harrogate, Michael Heelis's wife, Judith, showed a Herdwick gimmer, which won its class, was the female champion, and reserve overall Herdwick champion. Sadly Geoff Storey died suddenly not very long after the opening of the gallery, taking with him the secret of where Willie's and Beatrix's ashes had been scattered by his father.

One of the last fragments of Beatrix's writing seems an appropriate epitaph to them all:

> I will go back to the hills again
> when the day's work is done
> and set my hands against the rocks
> warm with an April sun
> and see the night creep down the fells
> and the stars climb one by one.